Late Boomers

Inspiring Stories About People Who've
Done Life-Changing Things Later in Life.

Jeri Bernstein

ISBN #9798665691947

First Edition

Printed in the United States

Cover photo: Taken by Samuel Furrer, Zoo Zurich, Switzerland

Acknowledgements

My heartfelt thanks to all the remarkable individuals featured in the book. Each of them so generously gave their time and their stories. By doing so, they also gave inspiration to people all over the world.

Dedicated to my husband, Louie, who has always been encouraging, helpful and pretty darn funny. And I like how he plays the guitar.

Table of Contents

Overcoming Obstacles.

How Ginny MacColl Re-shaped Her Life and Landed Healthier, Happier…and on Television.

When Ginny MacColl was 63, she decided to change her life by leaps and bounds.

Literally, leaps and bounds. She made a commitment to extreme fitness and a few years later, ended up jumping, vaulting and climbing as the oldest female contestant on NBC's TV show, American Ninja Warrior, Seasons 9 & 10. And she continues to compete in Regional and National Ninja League events.

If the notion of an in-her-late-60's Baby Boomer holding her own with 20-, 30- and 40-year-old world class athletes seems unbelievable, well, that's pretty much because Ginny *is* unbelievable. She's highly passionate, extremely dedicated and has more spunk and energy than most people half her age. And as she nears her seventh decade, she's lazar-focused on aging without limits and in the best of health. It all started with her burning desire to be stronger. And to do pull-ups.

"When I retired, I wanted to do all the things I didn't have time for before. We retired to Southport, (North Carolina) and I wanted to stay active. So, I joined the bike club, swim club, the kayak club, and got back to acting classes. I started taking yoga and Zumba, Pump It Up and cycle. I did everything and got so involved.

"But in addition to all my physical activity, I was finally free to travel and follow my daughter Jessie Graff, who has to date, gone farther than any other female on the finals of American Ninja Warrior."

The long-running television show is an action-packed series that follows extreme athletes who take on a series of seemingly impossible physical obstacles. On American Ninja Warrior, the contestants, who are both men and women and of varying ages, compete in different regions to qualify, then move on to City Finals. The winners of each city competition rise to the national stage and may even go on to compete internationally. Jessie (now a stunt actress,) who previously was involved in gymnastics, trapeze work, martial arts and pole vaulting, first appeared on the show in 2013. Her athletic life prepared her perfectly for these insanely challenging obstacle courses.

"As I'm watching her get involved in this, I'm watching her get strong. And she just looked *so* incredibly healthy. And it motivated me. I said, 'Jessie, I want to get stronger!' And her answer was, 'Well, Mom, do pull-ups.' "

"You know, I didn't have that kind of upper body strength. Women of my generation were never encouraged to lift weights. Muscle was sort of viewed as, well…unfeminine. Weights were totally new to me. And I didn't want to hurt myself. So, I got a personal trainer to help me. My goal was 5 pull-ups."

"After about seven months, people started commenting on how strong and toned I looked. It gave me such confidence, I wanted to keep doing it. And after an entire year of weight training, I finally got my first pull-up! It was so exciting."

But rather than rest on her physical laurels, Ginny wanted to do more. She worked her way to doing three pull-ups. Then five pull-ups. Stronger and gaining confidence, along with a growing admiration for her daughter and her fellow TV show contestants, she pushed (and pulled-up!) even more.

"I found out a local fellow who was previously on American Ninja Warrior, was building Ninja-like obstacles in his yard. He had built "Quintuple Steps", angled blocks set about four feet apart which you jump from one to the next. They were one of the original obstacles on the show. I got his permission to come try it out and I was hooked. I did it in 'baby steps.' I started with the steps closer together and little by little, was able to get through the obstacle, just like the athletes on TV. I sent a video to my daughter-and it sparked the concept of a mother/daughter duo on the show. So, I submitted an official audition video to the producers. You know, they get something like 70,000 audition videos each year! But I got in!"

If you look at her past, Ginny has been overcoming obstacles, metaphorically, all her life. She grew up in Knoxville, Tennessee, as she says "...as a pretty shy little soul." But her mother put her in dance classes that really brought her out of her shell. She became so passionate about dancing, she majored in dance in college. Then not-so-shyly-at-all, she headed for New York City. After working with some dance companies, she auditioned for and got a dancing role in the traveling version of the legendary Bob Fosse show, *Pippin*. When the show finished, Ginny understudied the role of Fastrada in New York and performed the lead in that role for two glorious weeks. Recalls Ginny, "It was such an exciting time of life. I was at the top of the top...on Broadway!"

Ginny then transitioned her career into doing TV commercials. Even though it was a totally new genre for her, in true Ginny fashion, she worked tirelessly and diligently and became a huge success. "I was lucky enough to have that 'mom' look they wanted at the time. I did all sorts of commercials...Jordache, Wonder

Bread, Folgers, Sizzlean. I did over 100 different commercials. It was a great time of life. A golden time." But as life would have it, it didn't last...due to another hurdle.

Her marriage failed and Ginny was left to raise her two kids alone. New York City wasn't the right place to do that. Nor was it possible to keep running out to auditions with the responsibilities of a single mom. She moved her family up to their lake house in the Poconos.

She worked several jobs at once (one as a dance teacher!) to make ends meet. Then she landed a solo job in local radio sales. And although the job was good, the remote mountain location proved to be yet another huge challenge. Says Ginny, "We lived deep in the woods. The kids' bus stop was a mile away. The weather conditions were so harsh. And whether it be shoveling snow, painting the house, the kids and I had to do everything ourselves. I learned that whatever the task, there was nobody else to do it, so I just had to do it. But it made me stronger." Seems like overcoming obstacles was a theme for her life.

Returning to the physical obstacles: Ginny *did* end up on American Ninja Warrior...twice! Remembers Ginny, "The first time, I fell on the first obstacle. I was devastated. But everyone, especially Jessie, supported me and picked me up. Jessie said, 'One fall doesn't define you! Look how far you've come.' And it was so true. So, as in my life, I learned to recover from my failure. Failures are just lessons. Through failure, we find strength. And I learned to believe in myself. And I went back on the show the next year."

Remarkable Ginny MacColl, the true-life warrior, continues to do Ninja-type competitions regionally and she swims competitively at events like the Senior Games, a national, Olympic-like competition for those over 50. But her audience has grown beyond those who marvel at her ageless physical abilities. She's now also passionately spreading the word to many senior gatherings about the great health benefits (both physical and mental) of fitness. She speaks to groups about staying active and getting stronger. And of course, Ginny herself is the perfect example of how age doesn't have to be limiting in any way. "Strength comes from within. The outer muscles show the mental strength, hard work and discipline to get here. Much of life is getting over our mental obstacles! She says, "Strong is the new healthy. And the new beautiful."

Ginny MacColl is both.

What advice would you give to Baby Boomers about starting a fitness program?

"It's all about baby steps. I tell people who haven't done anything before to start with walking. Make attainable goals. Start three times a week, 20 minutes at a time. Work on getting the heart rate up with intermittent fast walking and walk a little further each week. Be sure to add weight training or resistance training but invest in an instructor to learn proper techniques. This will help increase bone density which is imperative as we age! And, you know, our muscles do not age, as long as we use them!

"I would also say, believe in your dreams and go after them with all your heart and soul. Believe in yourself...that you can accomplish whatever you set your mind to. Train your mind to wear down your obstacles, excuses and fears!

"So, find your passion, make it a habit...be consistent, and grow from there. There's nothing more important than investing in your health.

"And it really helps to have a workout partner or buddy. It makes it fun!"

What surprised you the most about your late-in-life fitness journey?

"How confident it has made me. Getting over an obstacle is such a sense of accomplishment. And the amount of support I get from the other Ninjas is phenomenal. A lot of them say to me, 'I wish my mom and dad would do this with me!' "

"I also never expected all the health benefits. I had Osteopenia—a pre-condition to Osteoporosis. About two years after I began my intense weight training, I went to get a bone density test. The change in my bone density—without medication—'was statistically significant' and back to normal. I am a living example of how great fitness and weight training is for your health."

Do you have a motto or a mantra?

"Yes! *Strength is Ageless*, and it's never too late to start! Also, I don't say 'I can't do that.' Instead say, 'I can't do that **YET!**' "

What are your fitness goals for the future?

"Well, I just want to keep getting stronger. And get those next couple of pull-ups, says Ginny. As of this writing, she's up to 15! "And I'd like to compete again on American Ninja Warrior, probably next year." No surprise there!

Who would play you in "Overcoming Obstacles—The Movie?"

"Well, I would play myself!

"When I retired, I went back to acting and landed a role in the Movie, "Poms" with Diane Keaton. Her character goes to a retirement community and forms a cheerleading club of women all over 67 years old. It's a moving yet funny movie with an underlying theme of 'age is just a number, follow your dreams, if at first you fail, train harder and push through to success, and find a great supportive community.' It's a lot like my real-life journey."

And yes, Ginny MacColl is a true star.

To watch Ginny's on-going journey, follow her on Instagram @ginnymaccoll.

A Funny Thing Happened on the New Jersey Turnpike...

The Amusing Story of Rich and Malynda Madzel.

Some folks think "retirement" is just a joke.

That is certainly the case with Rich and Malynda Madzel. After completing successful careers and selling a decades-old family business, this energetic couple laughed at the thought of living a quiet, sedate, unproductive life. So, they started a stand-up comedy club.

"We were driving from our home in Columbia, Maryland, to Brooklyn to see our daughter," recalls Rich. "When I drive, I do a lot of thinking. I started saying to myself 'what could I be doing...?' I was a little bored. I really wanted to give back to the Columbia community. But cleaning bedpans at a hospital was really not my vision of the future.

"Then it occurred to me that Columbia didn't have a comedy venue that I knew of. Right there on the Jersey Turnpike, I thought, 'That's it! I'm going to start a comedy club! I'll call it *Try It Out Comedy*!' (At which point, my wife said, 'Oh boy, here we go...') I had the whole business model worked out before we reached our exit!" The fact that the Madzels had *never been* to a comedy club in their lives didn't damper the enthusiasm. And that, in itself, is pretty funny.

This particular Jersey Turnpike brainstorm session wasn't Rich's first. "When I don't have a project to work on, I get restless. And I get in trouble," he says. After retiring from the computer-end of Motorola, he joined the thriving marketing business Malynda had started. When the couple sold that, it wasn't like either of them to sit around. Malynda had, for years, been very active in the Columbia community...so much so that her legacy now resides in the Howard County Women's Hall of Fame and Maryland's Top 100 Women Circle of Excellence!

On an earlier Madzel road trip, Rich came up with a company called *Try It Out Theatre*. It was a format that showcased new playwrights—they would get a chance to write and read short, 10-minute plays in front of a live audience and get critiqued. The project was quite the hit, producing more than 100 performances and lasting for many years. Says Malynda, "Ask my husband if he's ever had any training as a playwright. Never mind, I'll answer that for you: No." Sounds like typical, fearless, Rich Madzel style...nothing stops him when he gets an idea.

"From *Try It Out Theatre*, I had learned the basic tasks," recalls Rich. "I knew how to get talent, get an audience and put on a production. I felt that the comedy club would be the same process, just a different topic!"

Rich leaned on his previous experience. But he also sought out some expertise from some people he wasn't familiar with, because *they* were familiar with comedy. He went online and found a web site about comedy clubs. The author owned a comedy club in Bethesda, MD. So, of course the Madzels headed out on yet another road trip.

"This guy, Curt Shackleford, produces probably the best club in the D.C. area. I said 'Curt, 'I'm going to start a comedy club, especially for new comics.' He gave me a lot of great advice and continues to, to this day.

"I also picked the brain of one of his senior comics, Robert Mac, a nationally-known comic who was performing the night we were there. He has since become my mentor for dealing with the art of comedy and the comics. With this initial advice, I was off and running."

"What I learned was, that in a comedy club, you want food and drink. So, I set my shows up in a restaurant, a really high-end, well-respected restaurant and supper club in downtown Columbia called Cured/18th & 21st. We wrote a plan and discussed it with the restaurant's owner. It was our job to get people into the restaurant with the show. It was his job to serve the people so well, they would become regulars.

"We committed to three shows, each on the first Monday of the month. We agreed that after three months, we would evaluate if it's working or not working." Well, the results were resounding--it not only worked, it *really* worked.

"In no time at all, I sold out those first three shows. So, we went ahead and booked shows for the entire year. These days, I sell 70 seats, *every* seat, two months in advance, in less than 48 hours. I have some people who come to every show."

The success of *Try It Out Comedy*, is not a surprise. What the Madzels enthusiastically serve up to their sold-out audiences (and the town of Columbia!) is a whole night of unique, up-lifting entertainment. It starts with a gourmet dinner at 5:30. After a crowd warm-up by Rich himself, the comics come on and perform for two hours, starting at 7:00. There are eight to ten comics per show. Some have traveled as much as three hours to get just three minutes on stage! They're new comics, up-and-comers and seasoned TV-performing professionals. Rich says, "The comics love working there. They get a good meal. They get paid. And they appreciate they are not in the basement of some seedy bar."

And the *Try It Out Comedy* performers are of every age, color and creed. Says Rich, "One comic is a 72-year old female Federal Appellate Judge. I have a retired New York City Judge. Probably because of the Columbia area, we see a lot of attorneys. I've had accountants perform. Motivational speakers. One of my favorites is a 15-year old girl. She's fantastic, very talented. I've had her back several times. Her whole family comes to support her. I really love that."

The Madzels not only love their diverse set of performers, they truly love what they do. They divide their tasks and work together seamlessly, a skill they acquired from their old marketing company days. It's been an enjoyable and inspiring ride...and it all worked, on so many levels. "It is wonderful all the joy *Try It Out Comedy* brings. It's rewarding providing the comics with a place to work. We provide the audience a nice place to come and a nice night out."

Says Rich, "Since doing *Try It Out Comedy*, we have learned that stand-up comedy is an art form like no other. It is truly 'working without a net.' Other performers have accompanists, back-up singers or dancers behind them. Stand-up comics only have themselves and a microphone. They must get the audience to like them and they have to practice for years before they get really good. It's amazing to see them work."

Malynda adds, "Giving back to the community has been the most important thing to me. The Columbia community has been very good to us. And I feel, with *Try it Out Comedy*, we are really giving back. We offer people something they enjoy doing, it's not far from their home, and best of all, they feel really good when they leave. They walk out of the show and tell me how much they enjoyed it and how they look forward to coming back. That is the ultimate reward to me—making people in Columbia happy."

Rich and Malynda are also pleasantly stunned by how it's effected their adult children. "They see us productive, self-sufficient, healthy and doing things." Malynda says, "My daughter now calls us 'badass!' I like that."

With *Try It Out Comedy*, Rich and Malynda Madzel started something new, different and something amazing that truly energized them. Says Malynda, "It's really just given us a new lease on life. I'm sure it's added years to our lives. We are so appreciative of it all."

'Funny how it all turned out.

What is one of the most surprising things about starting *Try It Out Comedy*?

Rich says, "I didn't realize, that because of *Try It Out Comedy,* I can now be silly! I was never known as a silly guy. Now I walk around in red florescent sneakers!"

What is the hardest part about *Try It Out Comedy*?

"It's simple—the hardest part is telling people it's sold out and they can't come. And telling comics, they can't be part of the show because it's already booked. It's really hard, because these are great comics, great people. And it's not fun telling someone 'You can't play,'" laments Rich.

What is the funniest story about your comedy story?

Malynda: "Unfortunately, I ended up in the emergency room for eight and a half hours. No food. No drinks. They finally take care of me. So, as I'm finally checking out, exhausted, a young physician's assistant, asks us, 'Are you retired?" We said no, we run a comedy club. He stops taking my information, midstream, turns around and starts auditioning his comedy routine!"

What is in the future for *Try It Out Comedy*?

Both Madzels agree, "As long as the audiences keep coming and the comics keep asking to perform, we'll keep producing shows. We will also keep the standards we have set for having a great venue and 'clean' material."

What's your best advice?

Rich says, "Just get out there and do whatever it is you want to do. Don't tell me you're 80-years old and you can't."

Who would play you in "Try It Out Comedy—The Movie?"

Rich: "I think Al Pacino. He can play the epitome of a Brooklyn guy, which is who I am."

Without hesitation, Malynda responds: "Alfre Woodard." Sounds like she's thought about this before...

Rich can be reached at RMadzel@hotmail.com.

And Malynda at ctsprez@hotmail.com.

Let the Good Times Roll.

Andree Kehn's Winning Bout with Roller Derby.

Andree Kehn has one of the most interesting and diverse life resumes that one can imagine. She's been a successful wedding photographer, a ski bum, an army brat, a carnie, a motorcycle rider, a lifeguard, a tour director, an organic gardener and a producer of highly creative, fascinating, underwater art. She's currently employed as a photojournalist in Maine. But in recent years, into her fifth decade, she added yet another facet to her remarkably impressive life: She joined a roller derby league.

"I work as a photographer for a local newspaper," says Andree. "A few years ago, at a regular daily staff meeting, where we talk about what is going in the paper in the coming week, someone brought up that the Maine Roller Derby organization was actively trying to change some old and odd legislation that hindered their sport. I volunteered to take the photos for the story."

When she went out to her assigned job, Andree learned a lot more about roller derby and also learned what great, open-minded and welcoming people the team members were. "They kept saying, 'You should join us! C'mon, join us!' And they were saying all that despite the fact that I didn't know how to roller skate, I wasn't in great shape and well...I was OLD!"

But, because the team was so outgoing and encouraging, Andree took them up on their offer. She joined "The Inferno" a team which is part of The Androscoggin Fallen Angels Roller Derby League. And with that, she found a whole new family of friends and yet another new passion in life. These days, a few years later,

Andree (derby name: Photo Bomber) is one of the team's blockers. She's in charge of the team's training program and has worked on marketing, ticketing and publicity behind the scenes, 10-15 hours a week. Not to mention, she is probably one of the most enthusiastic roller derby supporters on the entire east coast.

Right from the get-go, she had an inkling that her participation in roller derby would lead to much more than just honing her athletic skills and learning how to skate. For Andree, this new interest proved to be not just a novel physical endeavor that would improve her fitness and confidence, but roller derby offered unexpected social benefits, as well. Andree knew that roller derby, for the most part, is a woman's sport. But what she came to learn was because of that, there's a unique culture and camaraderie. "The sport appeals to a lot of feminists. There's a lot of acceptance. There's a mindset of embracing women, wherever they may be in their lives."

She goes on, "Because of the peculiarity of the sport, new team members often have never felt 'athletic' or played on a team, and everyone accepts that. There is definite non-judgmental support and a group effort to help each team member in their own journey to being more athletic and being part of a team sport. And each team member is encouraged to play the position they want. All the other team members help them get there."

Andree also found out that roller derby had women of *every* age. While most of her teammates are in their 20's and 30's, there are women, like her, in their 50's...even 60's! Andree goes on,
"One of the things I really love, is there is no agism in this sport. Our team, The Inferno, actually publishes everyone's birthday on our website, just for that reason. I mean, I'm twice the age of some of these women, but it's not an obstacle. I am great friends

with women in their 20's! And where else would that ever happen?!"

Andree finds that roller derby is not only open to participation of every age, but the sport, in general, is very open to every shape. She claims, "Roller derby is amazing in its all-over acceptance of all sizes of women. It's very 'body-positive.' No one is ever forced to feel bad about their weight. Some players are large women. But they're amazingly athletic. And largeness and athleticism aren't normally thought of as good things in women's sports. It's just so nice that people are appreciated for what size they are and how they contribute to the team."

As rewarding as roller derby has been for Andree, the sport definitely has its hard knocks. Seriously, hard knocks. The play is extremely physical, aggressive and competitive. As any roller derby participant, Andree has had her share of bumps, bruises and broken bones. But even with those injuries, the sport has given Andree much more than it's literally hurt. While many people her age are physically winding down, Andree is out there blocking, hip-whipping and plowstopping with the best of them. It's given her confidence. Strength. Athletic prowess. And best of all, a true community of support and great friends.

Let's just say, at this stage of life, Andree Kehn is on a great roll.

Was there any push-back from friends or family when you decided to join roller derby?

"It was a tough transition, but they are all excited for me now. At first, my family wasn't so thrilled, because I got hurt a few times.

But they all see now how much joy it has brought into my life, so they've come around."

What advice would you give to someone considering joining the sport?

"The motto is, 'You're never too old or too out-of-shape to start playing roller derby!'"

Did anything about joining a roller derby team really surprise you?

"Well, it was really different than I thought it would be. I was surprised by the incredible sense of community. I've found some of the closest friends of my lifetime. And the cross-age bonding. To be able to make such close friendship with people so much younger than me is profound."

"It was also a surprise to learn that having a big butt would be really admirable!"

Has being in roller derby changed you as a person?

"Yes. I've gotten a lot less hard on myself. It taught me that nothing is perfect and some days you just get out there and do the best you can. It's all a journey…"

Do you wish you made this decision to join a roller derby team earlier in life?

"Oh, absolutely! I'm probably not going to get to an all-star level at this age. And it would have been pretty cool to have done that."

Which Hollywood stars would play you in "Andree the Roller Derby Queen--The Movie?"

Andree quickly answers, "Meryl Streep." We all know this gifted actress is well-adept at making memorable hits...let's just hope she's able to take some!

Photograph of Andree courtesy of Ram Sports.

Tails from the Road.

How a Two Time Former "CFO of the Year" Put Retirement in the Rearview Mirror and Started Saving Dogs.

Everyone who knows Charlie Kleman would readily agree that he is a driven man. *Really* driven. How else would one reach such impressive and plentiful achievements and career highs? After working on public offerings at the then largest CPA firm in the world, his third try as CFO at taking a company public was successful as he, and the management team he helped develop, grew one of his companies (a retailer) from $6 million in sales with 12 company owned stores to $1.2 billion and over 1,200 stores! At that company, the values skyrocketed, and the stock became known as the 'Darling of Wall Street' and the 'Stock of the Decade' as pronounced in 2006 by the Wall St. Journal.

Charlie is a smart-as-a-whip, business-savvy, immensely ambitious guy. But in his retirement years, Charlie made a huge U turn. Rather than being driven, he became a driver. Sometimes his passengers snarl at him. Sometimes they greet him with a big sloppy kiss. Although his riders' disposition may vary, the one thing they all have in common is four legs and a tail.

Charlie became a volunteer dog transporter for Atlanta Lab Rescue, taking dogs all over the southeast, from high-kill shelters to the refuge of foster homes or safety of welcoming kennels. But leave it to this life-long overachiever to not do anything half-heartedly. Charlie Kleman travels with his furry transports to-the-tune-of 36,000 miles a year! Since he started his car rides in 2015, he has saved over 2,000 dogs.

"I love doing this," beams Charlie. "I have a lot of fun, so for me, there's no effort at all." Charlie's daily docket may have him picking up a rescue from the other side of the city or the other side of the state. He may bring the dog from a shelter to someone's home or he may bring a sick dog back and forth to the vet. He may be picking up a dog that is being surrendered by its owner or being given back by its foster. Sometimes his job is transporting a dog from an awful circumstance to its wonderful forever home.

Charlie's riders may be dogs he knows nothing about. Or dogs he knows only too well. "One dog named Clifford, I transported 25 times!" recalls Charlie. "He was very protective of his fosters and would become aggressive if another person got close to them. But the story ended happily. He found a home on a farm. The owner *wanted* Clifford to protect him. He's doing great." This makes Charlie smile.

Clifford was one dog Charlie remembers easily. But there are thousands of others, all of which he has chronicled in a three-ring binder he keeps in his car. He transports as many as five dogs a day. "It's really a full-time job," he says. "I am out almost every single day. It might be for an hour one day, or it might be for 10 hours. The other day, I did about 660 miles." Needless to say, he's a doggone hero.

During his childhood and his remarkable run in the corporate world, Charlie always liked dogs and often owned one. But one canine in particular, a Lab named Kandi, really changed his life, later in life. With the help of his daughter, a cardiologist veterinarian, he and his wife rescued Kandi when she was on the brink of being euthanized. The Klemans doted on Kandi for the next 14 ½ years. When she died, Charlie vowed he would dedicate his life to saving dogs like her. That's when he "knocked on the door" of Atlanta Lab Rescue. And in the same way he operated all his whole life, he was all in.

Currently, Charlie chairs the board of the rescue organization. He does the bookkeeping and he's a more-than-generous fundraiser and donor that is determined to build the organization to a level that will assure its long-term existence. But the car rides are what truly drive his passion and his heart. He remarks, "I do the bulk of the transport for the organization. I started in my Jaguar in 2015, but that was too small for the giants I sometimes had and I could only handle one dog at a time!" (Some of his first rescues were literally lucky dogs!) "Now I have a Land Rover that has been custom-fitted with crates in the back." Not that all the dogs Charlie drives ride in a crate. Says Charlie, "I've had dogs get in the car and hide under the front seat and won't come out. I have dogs that just insist that they are going to sit on my lap while I'm driving and I have had many pregnant ones that I prayed would hold off until I got them to a vet!"

But no matter how the ride starts out, it just about always ends calmly. Charlie has a gentle, pacifying effect on even the most terrified animal. He says, "I never had any real dog training, and I don't know why, but the dogs love me. I think they pick up on my energy and know I'm here to help. When you put them in the car, they sense they're being rescued. You can see the happiness and appreciation in their eyes growing as they begin to realize their life is changing… and for the better!"

While transporting dogs can be a touching and rewarding venture, it can be a messy one as well. Reports Charlie, "About 30% of the dogs either throw up or poop or pee in my car. Many of them have never ever been in a car! And I've had some break their stitches and bleed. A lot of hair is everywhere. And some really bad smells! But we clean it up and move to the next one!"

But despite the untidiness, transporting dogs has meant the world to Charlie. "It's very satisfying saving dogs. It gives me a purpose. And I feel I'm doing something that really makes a difference." But it works both ways. Volunteering at Atlanta Lab Rescue has made a difference in Charlie, too. "I look forward to getting up every morning. I love when I get a call that there's a dog to pick up. I get on the road and it makes my day." For the 500+ dogs that Charlie transports every year, that ride not only makes their day, it saves their lives. And these days, Charlie Kleman is not only driven by this, he's moving full speed ahead.

Did anything about becoming the world's most ambitious dog transporter surprise you?

"I am surprised at how much I've learned about dogs. I'm surprised at how much I thought I knew, but I really didn't know."

What was the hardest part about being a volunteer transporter at Atlanta Lab Rescue?

"Not having time for doing other things I enjoy. This really is a fulltime job. But it's a job I love and I wouldn't have it any other way!"

What is in the cards (or should we say 'cars') for your future?

"I just want to keep doing what I'm doing. I am very satisfied with my life, both as CFO, parent and dog rescuer."

If "Charlie the Famous Dog Transporter" ever becomes a Hollywood movie, who would play you?

"Maybe Paul Newman," Charlie says. Well, seeing as Mr. Newman was aptly behind the wheel in a race car movie called "Winning," and a real-life race car driver himself, he might be just the right choice.

Support Charlie's driving cause by donating at
AtlantaLabRescue.com

Super Hero.

The Colorful Story of How
Bill Zimmerman Used Comic Books to Teach Students All Over
the World.

As a child, Bill Zimmerman was obsessed with comics. He *devoured* them. 'Matter of fact, he rarely had a meal without a comic book next to his plate! His favorite day of the week was Sunday, when his father would venture out of their Brooklyn home and return with breakfast and an armful of newspapers. "I would grab the papers from him and pull out the comic sections," recalls Bill. "I fell in love with the color and the characters. Comic strips allowed me to enter a new world."

Bill feels that the comics not only taught him how to read, it gave him and enormous dose of creativity and inventiveness. But as big as his imagination grew, he could have never imagined that his early zealous fascination would lead to him, in his retirement, to developing a remarkable website called MakeBeliefsComix, where you can create your own comic strips online. It's a robust site that teaches reading, new languages, innovation and problem solving through the use of nearly one hundred cartoon characters and settings. The interactive, highly engaging site is translated into over 30 languages and has visitors from every corner of the globe. Funny, how with his beloved "funnies," Bill achieved his dream of 'giving back' and helping others by teaching and hundreds of thousands of students each month for free.

Bill's comic-fueled imagination has served him well throughout his life and his career. While he toyed with illustration and art classes, he ended up becoming an extraordinary newspaper journalist ("Because I loved newspapers so much...") and rose to become the editor in chief at American Banker and then Newsday. During his years in the industry, it was a time when newspapers were turning to graphics and color to enhance the news stories. You can imagine, with his visual upbringing and love for color, Bill jumped on the trend immediately. He incorporated brilliant charts and graphs...and even a cartoon or two. "When I started working for Newsday, which was one of the largest tabloids at the time, I had a lot of creative freedom. I introduced a unique feature called the Student Briefing Page, in order to teach young people about current events. It ran for 13 years and was syndicated all over the country. It was one of the most gratifying projects of my career." This page was a true one-of-a-kind. It not only used engaging graphics to present the information, it was interactive, prompting the reader to grab a pencil and participate, whether it was writing in the answer to a compelling question or filling in conversation bubbles over the cartoon heads of world leaders. One wonders what possibly compelled Bill to create that?! The page was twice nominated for a Pulitzer Prize.

Always yearning for creative outlets, Bill decided to run the newspaper by day, and write books at night. Not mysteries or historic novels, but rather books for kids. Books that would teach and support their young lives and encourage their voices. Most importantly and uniquely, books that made the reader a true participant.

To start the process, he collaborated with a graphic artist he had met at the newspaper, a cartoonist named Tom Bloom. "My first book" says Bill, "was called *Make Beliefs. A Book for your Imagination.* I created the text and then Tom would add an illustration."

Still in print today, the book is a series of fun and thought-provoking prompts, to be completed by the reader with pencil or crayon. The question-answer format engages the reader and allows them to tap into fresh ideas and new thinking. The reader can also color the drawings, allowing each individual to create a personalized book all their own. With Tom Bloom's help, Bill quickly finished and self-published three more books and sold them to Bantam. He would go on to write more than two dozen books, all interactive, featuring writing prompts. The books have been featured on the Today Show and PBS. His written work has been featured in The New York Times, The Wall Street Journal and in magazines such as Family Circle, Parents, Esquire and Business Week.

In 2004, when Bill Zimmerman left the newspaper world, he walked away from amazing accomplishments and contributions as well as an illustrious 42-year career. But there was no way he was leaving behind his life's passion: creativity. And his mission to contribute to society and to "do good." Through his book writing and newspaper experience, he knew the comic book "format" was a great way to connect with children. It was friendly, bite-sized, colorful and fun. "So, I decided to build a free website where students could make their own comic strips and learn reading and writing in the process," recalls Bill. In 2006, he launched MakeBeliefsComix.com. So far, the site has had 22 million visitors.

Like many of the creations Bill has gifted the world, MakeBeliefsComix.com is interactive and makes it easy to create comic strips, greeting cards, e-books and more. On the site, users can choose from dozens of diverse comic characters: they are of all ages and races. There are characters with disabilities. Some characters are based on humans or animals. Some are just based on Bill's limitless imagination!

Since its launch, MakeBeliefsComix has had visits from over 200 countries. The text is offered in more than 30 languages. In addition to children, educators have been the site's biggest fans, using it to as a tool to teach writing, reading and to teach another language. Wanting it to be a useful resource, MakeBeliefsComix offers lesson plans for teachers and even has a special section for teaching special education. "We found a lot of special needs educators find that working with our comic book format is very useful in communicating with autistic children. Some that don't use their voices much can express things that are troubling them through the use of the characters and settings," says Bill.

Although the site was conceived to serve children, people of all ages find it useful and fun. It's a perfect platform for parents to connect with their children and a great vehicle for grandparents to stay in touch with grandkids who may live a distance away. It provides a great way for business people to de-stress from work. Activities and social directors use it for inspiration.

MakeBeliefsComix was an endowment to everyone. But it was also important to Bill. "It was really a gift to myself," reflects Bill. "I wanted a project that would enhance my life and help people. I hope the website touches people in some way and changes their lives. I will never make a fortune on it, though!" But, MakeBeliefsComix is a truly priceless addition to the world.

These days, aside from managing MakeBeliefsComix, Bill still reads the comics. "I still do it every day. I still love getting lost in the comic world. It's probably the finest 5-10 minutes of my day. Comics are just so beautiful, and I like the fantasy. Everything is possible."

Well, Bill made it possible. Thanks to his vision, his passion, his imagination and his love of comics, people everywhere are taught and touched by his amazing MakeBeliefsComix.com. Bill is a wonderful, inspiring example how you're never too old to make a meaningful impact. He 'makes belief-ers' of us all.

Was there anything creating MakeBeliefsComix.com that surprised you?

"I didn't realize the internet could be so exciting. It gives you so much power to reach people and help people. Some of my books were successful and that is very gratifying. But with the website, I can reach hundreds of thousands of people each month."

Do you think you could have created MakeBeliefsComix.com earlier in your life?

"No. During my years as a newspaper editor, I had thoughts of it. But there were too many deadlines and I was too busy. I needed the free time of my retirement to get my ideas together. I am really grateful for these years when I can continue to learn and explore things.

What's in the future of MakeBeliefsComix.com? And you!?

"I will keep trying to enhance the site. When we started, we had 8 characters. Now we have 60-70 characters! We keep adding characters and new features. As for me, well I'm always happiest when I'm creating something. So now, I'm working on a new book with Tom Bloom, the illustrator. This book will encourage readers to have conversations with their pets!" That sounds like classic Zimmerman imagination.

If "The Creation of MakeBeliefsComix.com" becomes a Hollywood movie, who would play you?

When answering this, as always, Bill thinks outside the box. "I think the cartoon that represents me on the website would play me. I mean, he IS me." If the movie ever happens, one thing we will all know for certain: Bill Zimmerman is a real character.

You can access Bill's remarkable site at <u>MakeBeliefsComix.com</u>.

Contact Bill himself at <u>billz@makebeliefscomix.com</u>.

Mother of Invention.

How Lou Childs Invented an Ingenious Baby Product That Succeeded Swimmingly.
(And Even Drew the Attention of Sharks.)

Everyone knows that the world's most successful inventions are born to solve a problem or fill a need. And, Lou Childs, a Columbus, Georgia resident, had both. The mother of six grown children, she had them all over to her house for Christmas, not all that long ago. Several of them and their spouses were staying for a few nights so they could spend the holiday together. It was a special year because the family was being joined by Lou's first granddaughter. Recalls Lou, "Katy is my oldest child and was there with her husband and her 7-month-old daughter, Margot. Because there were so many of us there, everybody had to share rooms. The baby was used to having her own, dark, private bedroom. But in this situation, Margot was put to bed in her porta-crib, in the same room with her parents. She could see them and was confused. And there was unfamiliar light coming in from the windows." The baby couldn't sleep. So, neither did her parents. Or anyone else in the household, for that matter. Miserable from the lack of rest, Katy and her family left.

The whole family was so disappointed. And tired! Lou continues, "When Katy got home, I called her and I said, there has got to be a solution for this. People share rooms all the time, like on vacation. We've got to figure this out." And, boy, did they ever. They were innovative. They were determined. Most importantly, they were successful. And they ended up on TV on ABC's Shark Tank.

31

Lou never set out to be a game-changing inventor. But, she says, looking back on it however, everything that happened in her life had clearly led up to this point. She says, "It gives me goosebumps to think of how this all played out so beautifully."

Born to an amazingly resilient, nose-to-the-grindstone woman, who was widowed when Lou was just three, Lou witnessed her mother working wisely, tirelessly and never complaining. "She had five children to raise on her own," says Lou. "Yet, despite that, she went back to college and got her master's degree in teaching and a certificate that was like a doctorate degree. She was a very, very strong woman and that's what she taught me to be."

Lou found herself in a similar situation about a decade and a half after she dropped out of college. She already had four children and was unfortunately left to provide for them on her own. It was a challenging situation, but drawing from her mother's strength, Lou went back to college and a month before her 40th birthday she got a degree in corporate journalism from Auburn University.

With her new credentials, Lou held an impressive array of marketing jobs, ranging from small companies to Fortune 500 firms. She acquired an outstanding set of marketing and product development skills. After decades of working, she got a phone call from the CEO of her then current company and was laid off. As crushing as this was, Lou realized for the first time in decades, she had time on her hands. This happened not long after the Christmas sleep fiasco at her home. "I said to my daughter, if we're going to get serious about creating this product, now is the time." Aside from the fact that Lou's daughter Katy now had a two-year old, a demanding full-time job and was two weeks away from delivering twins, Katy agreed. Determination and fearlessness are obviously part of the family DNA.

Not only did they get down to the business of inventing a product that would help a baby sleep soundly in a strange environment, they approached the task wisely and with careful calculation. "Every job I ever had fed into that moment. Says Lou. "I had been in product development. I'd been in business communication. I'd been in marketing and software development. All of my experiences made it the perfect storm of opportunity." Lou goes on, "I took an accelerator class for entrepreneur start-ups, which taught me soup-to-nuts what I needed to get done to launch a product. We then enlisted the help of a product development shop to help with the physical design." After several on-paper concepts and then two actual prototypes, SlumberPod^R was born.

SlumberPod is a one-of-a-kind portable sleep nook that fits over a play pen or travel crib, sort of like a lightweight tent. While it blocks the vision and light for the baby sleeping inside, it doesn't "hug" the crib making it feel claustrophobic. The area inside is a totally breathable, moveable environment. It's easily assembled and easily moved as it folds into its own carry-on bag with a shoulder strap. It also easily allows for a good night's sleep for a baby or anyone sharing a room with the baby, anywhere.

The product was launched in July of 2018, with a manufacturer's order of 500. Thanks to the support of Kickstarter and a savvy use of Facebook, SlumberPod sold out all units and Lou and Katy had to order 2,000 more. By December 2018—just five months after launching, SlumberPod earned $100,000. (And a lot of parents earned some good sleep!)

In February 2019, on a whim, Lou and Katy thought they'd take their story to Shark Tank, a very popular television series that allows entrepreneurs to pitch their products and businesses to a panel of famous financial tycoons ("sharks") in order to get investment dollars. Lou and her daughter flew to Dallas for their casting call, which was a 1 minute, 30 second presentation of SlumberPod. "When we got there," recalls Lou, "We were in line with at least 400 other entrepreneurs. For Shark Tank auditions, that's actually a short line!

"They warn you at the beginning about the process. They said, 'We may engage with you, we may seem interested, but that doesn't mean you're going to the next round.' We were lucky enough to get to pitch to one of the most senior producers. She seemed to be very interested, but you never know. We had to go through several other stages of screening, but we finally got the call. We were going to be on Shark Tank."

On January 5, 2020, Lou and Katy's episode of Shark Tank aired nationally to an audience of millions. The two women, clad in pink pajamas and shark-shaped slippers, gave a truly winning, captivating television presentation. Not only did SlumberPod get exposed to the world, it got funded. Shark Barbara Corcoran agreed fully to Lou and Katy's proposed deal.

"It was a blast," beams Lou. "They were all extremely nice. It went soooo well. Except when Mr. Wonderful (one of the sharks) said, 'How much is Slumber *PRISON*?' But it made us laugh."

These days, with projected sales for 2020 to be hovering at $4 million, Lou is at the helm of the company, as COO. After a stellar marketing career, she didn't retire, but took her professional life to the next level, by creating a wonderful, helpful product and becoming a wildly successful entrepreneur. Lou Childs. Along with her daughter Katy, 'concepted", designed and created SlumberPod to solve a problem or fill a need. But the truth is, the remarkable invention was Lou herself.

Was there anything about you turning into an inventor and launching a product surprised you?

"It totally surprised me how all these different things just fell into place."

Did you get advice from other entrepreneurs?

"Oh yes. The entrepreneurial world is so giving. They all want to help you. We had a great network of people to tap into. And that was really important for our success."

What do you think was the hardest part about your whole SlumberPod experience?

"Well, maybe keeping a secret about being on Shark Tank. You know, you are sworn to secrecy and can't say a word about it until two weeks before your episode airs. I didn't even tell my husband about it. When we went to LA to film, I told him we were going to a baby show. He didn't find out about it until he saw us on TV!"

Do you think you could have launched SlumberPod earlier in your life?

"I think it came at the perfect time. Everything that I have done in life up until the launch, set me up for success. I don't know if I would have been ready earlier."

What's in your future?

"I am going to continue to run the company and we are launching some new products. We're going to launch a SlumberPod that goes
over a pet crate. As well as a full-size crib version for babies to use every day at home."

If "The Invention of the SlumberPod" becomes a Hollywood movie, who would play you and Katy?

"Well, I think maybe Jamie Lee Curtis or Annette Bening could play me. And Katy could be played by Sarah Jessica Parker." 'Don't know if any of those actresses ever worked together, but if they did, it's bound to be a great success.

To learn more about Slumberpod and Lou's fantastic encounter with Sharks, go to slumberpod.com.

Real Estate Remix.

How DJ Jimmy Baron left the entertainment world and put a great new spin on his life.

As someone who made having breakfast with David Bowie or dinner at Elton John's place all part of the job, Jimmy Baron had a pretty idyllic career. Jimmy was in the radio business for 23 years, and for 13 of those years was part of a dynamic drivetime radio trio (and sometimes duo) who dominated the airwaves on a highly influential morning show in Atlanta. Because the show had a then-breakthrough format which included having notable guests in the studio, he got to hob-knob with the hottest musicians and shoot the breeze with celebrities. Heck, he even had a sit-down with the Dalai Lama! When it all came to a sudden halt just a few days before his 50th birthday, how in heaven's name would Jimmy cue up a new career? Well, he became a real estate rock star, of course.

"There is absolutely nothing in my background would indicate that real estate would be in my future," says Jimmy. As a matter of fact, after his radio fall-out his mother suggested he give real estate a shot and he told her, "...it was the worst idea she ever had." Jimmy adds, "But early in my life, there was *every* indication that radio would be a good choice for me, which it turned out it was."

Even as a kid, Jimmy was drawn towards entertainment. Says Jimmy, "I was always the class clown. I wasn't really into academics." Although in high school, he was a high achiever in other things such as sports and being on the stage, starring in school plays. Because of that, to no one's surprise and to his parents' dismay, Jimmy skipped college, and at age 17, headed off to California to be an actor.

Like many wannabe stars, Jimmy started out his life in L.A. with the glamourous job of driving a cab. But he got his "foot-in-the-door" to the acting world by getting into the Screen Extras Guild. He started making a living as a TV and movie "extra". He recalls, "I was an extra on many, many shows. It wasn't a bad way to make money, but nobody goes from an extra to a leading role as an actor. So, I got an agent and started going out on auditions. And I had some success." Seeing as Jimmy landed roles in movies including *Risky Business, The Sure Thing* and *Heart Like a Wheel,* and parts in television shows such as *M*A*S*H*, Facts of Life* and *Quincy*, one would re-describe his so-called "some" success to "much" success. But he says, "I was able to get enough work to realize that wasn't what I actually wanted to do. But I got it out of my system." The bottom line was, this sort of entertainment didn't keep Jimmy entertained.

On a whim, Jimmy decided to take a night course at UCLA about cultivating a career in radio. "I spent so much of my cab-driving days listening to DJ's on the radio. I thought, yeah, I can do what these guys do." The teacher of the course was also a consultant to radio stations around the country and saw potential in Jimmy. He set up a few job interviews and Jimmy ended up as a radio producer. He started in San Diego, worked in Chicago for a bit then ended up in Atlanta as a producer for the morning show at a new, uniquely formatted radio station labelled 99X.

Jimmy had no intention of becoming a radio personality, but that's exactly what happened. "As the producer of the show, you are in the studio with the show hosts," explains Jimmy. "At 99X, the two morning hosts kept bringing me in on segments and bits. I just transitioned to becoming an on-air part of the show." And it turned out to be quite the show, at that.

Like everything in entertainment, being at the right place at the right time means everything. And 99X snagged both for Jimmy Baron. It was an alternative rock format and Atlanta happened to be one of the country's big hubs for that genre of music. The station became hugely influential not just in the city, but throughout the United States. The morning show Jimmy hosted with Steve Barnes and Leslie Fram became wildly popular, as the hosts were intuitively plugged into to pop culture.

Says Jimmy, "We were doing a lot of fun things no one else had ever tried before on the radio. Theater of the mind stuff. We interviewed people from all walks of life. We had a ton of creative leeway. It really struck a chord with the city."

The listeners loved the morning show at 99X. And the critics did, too. At one time, the show was one of the highest-rated shows on American alternative rock radio. It won numerous national and local awards. And Jimmy really loved the lifestyle and career he created.

"It was an AMAZING life to be leading back then," recalls Jimmy.
"We met *every* celebrity. Jane Fonda. Warren Beatty. Paul McCartney. You name it. We routinely were privileged to do so many once-in-a-lifetime things. We broadcast every year from the MTV Movie Awards and the Grammys. We even were the only station given the rights to broadcast live from the Coca-Cola Olympic Village during the 1996 games." Jimmy was part of all that 99X magic for 13 years.

Like many good things, it eventually was going to end. And that happened to Jimmy just days short of his 50th birthday. A different radio station that he was then working for, completely changed formats and everyone, including Jimmy, was fired.

"It was a gut punch. But I stepped back and realized, I had pretty much played out my radio career in Atlanta. I was going to have to do something else. But I had no idea what *that* was. Doing morning radio was a great career that helped you develop absolutely no transferrable skills. Nobody at UPS or Delta was looking to hire a guy who could tell jokes or give away concert tickets."

Jimmy's mother suggested he should get his real estate license. His reaction: "Don't ever say that to me again." But like a good son, he did listen. He took an online real estate course and was surprised how much he really liked it. And he was hungry to learn more.

"I think I liked it because it was such a departure from what I had done my entire life, yet it was something I understood. And I knew there was an opportunity to make a decent living at it."

A friend of Jimmy's, had a boutique real estate firm and welcomed Jimmy in. And Jimmy adapted well. He came to the realization that the radio world, where he had spent his last several decades, had provided him a valuable skill set after all. "I really enjoyed the human interaction," Jimmy reflects. "I liked getting to know different people and helping them solve problems. I spent the last 23 years trying to put a smile on people's faces, trying to make them laugh. Engaging them in conversation. All the things that made me a successful radio personality turned out to be very beneficial in real estate. I know how to communicate and make people feel good. Those traits are very important in sales."

And they really paid off. After about two years at the small firm, Jimmy moved to Keller Williams to tap into the vast resources and vibrant energy of the largest real estate firm in the world. The move did a world of good for Jimmy's career. There are about 550 real estate agents in the Keller Williams Sandy Springs (Georgia) office and in 2019 Jimmy Baron was the number one individual Realtor.

Says Jimmy, "Selling real estate was just such a great career move for me. After radio, I never thought I'd find another job that I would love so much and have so much fun." Today, Jimmy is energized, enthusiastic about his career and excited to face every day. It appears that Jimmy's new playlist is going to be around for a while.

Do you think you could have built a successful real estate career earlier in your life?

"No", Jimmy answers definitively. "In my 20's and 30's, I wanted to be the center of attention. I wanted to be the guy on the stage, to be an entertainer. And I loved it. But as I got older, those things became less important to me. I don't care about that anymore. Now, I care about helping people. And I love what I do."

What advice would you give to someone making a later-in-life, complete career change?

"You have to expand your mind and be open to ideas. We think we know what's best for ourselves, but sometimes people see you differently than you see yourself. And there's value to that."

He adds, "And you should always listen to your mother!"

What's in your future?

"I think I'll stay in real estate for the next 15 years. Early to mid-seventies is not as old as it used to be." Which happens to be exactly the point of the "Late Boomers" book!

If *The Jimmy Baron Story* becomes a Hollywood movie, who would play you?

"Michael J. Fox," is the reply. But maybe, because Jimmy has already graced the big screen a time or two, he can simply play himself!

Jimmy is committed to helping you make great real estate decisions that will improve the quality of your life. Contact him at Jimmy@JimmyBaron.com.

The Power to Make a Difference.

How Joe Power Elected to Opt Out of Retirement and Get into Politics.

Joe Power spent decades in a successful banking career outside of Washington D.C. Some of his clients included U.S. Senators and Congressmen, high-powered legal authorities. He loved the fast pace of the industry and the excitement of being at the heart of the nation's capital, a dynamic, bustling city. But when he and his wife Pam (who was also in the banking industry,) decided to retire, they thought they'd go someplace smaller, less hectic, where they could read, relax and maybe even renovate because they both have a love of history and architecture. But a calm, quiet life just wasn't in the cards. Because Joe ended up on a ballot.

"I was born in Talladega, Alabama, but never really
lived there. My parents were born and raised there, but we moved to Fairfax Virginia when I was just ten years old," recalls Joe. Despite not being raised there, the Powers were very familiar with the area, as they spent much time visiting their parents and stopping in the city on the way to their panhandle beach house. Joe goes on, "Pam really wanted to retire in Talladega. So, several years before I retired, we bought Sugar Hill." Sugar Hill is the name of a sprawling Colonial Cottage style home, built in 1835 and believed to be one of the oldest homes in the city. To see the home today, it's spectacular. But when Joe and Pam brought it, it was a spectacular wreck. "It was really beat up," says Joe. It became the Power's mission to restore the home and bring it back to its original beauty.

"In the middle of the Sugar Hill renovation," Joe remembers, "We received a cease and desist order. We were told we had to stop work on the outside of the house. The order was from Talladega's Historic Preservation Commission. I didn't even know what that was! Apparently, we didn't have the right permit to alter a historic structure. How was I supposed to know about that!?"

Upon taking his complaints to his home inspector, who agreed that the requirements for renovation in the city were complicated and somewhat pointless, he was given the advice, 'Well maybe you should change things. Maybe you should get involved.' Boy, did he ever!

Joe joined the Historic Preservation Commission. It wasn't long after, he became the president of the organization. (No surprise there.) He learned a boatload about historic preservation. But because it connected him to the local government, he also learned about the somewhat dysfunctional politics in this small southern city. "There was all kinds of arguing. Everyone was starting to sue everyone else. Suits, countersuits. It was not a very nice situation." Because of that, after a few years, Joe left the commission.

Getting this not-so-great inside look at local government, put a "bug in his bonnet" as Joe says. "I really did not like what was going on, especially at the City Council level. I thought, 'somebody's got to put a stop to all this foolishness.' My experience in D.C. banking connected me to many people in government...prominent Senators and Representatives. I could see, from them, what it would take to be a leader. And although I never dreamed this is where I would end up, I thought, 'I can do this.' I knew I was a better person than the incumbent. I knew I could do a better job. So, I ran for City Council. And Pam helped me."

The journey to election day was a wild and wooly ride. "You can't imagine how nasty these things can get," said Joe. But he jumped in with a level head and thick skin. "I started by putting together a bunch of people who also thought I could do a better job. We recruited an advisory board of twelve really smart people, a couple of whom lived in Talladega their whole life. My nextdoor neighbor became my campaign manager. She made literally hundreds of phone calls on my behalf. She got on that phone and just wouldn't stop. She hosted multiple events. She's always been very involved in the community and she really believed in me." If her dedication and relentless energy seem amazing, consider this: Joe's Campaign Manager, Idele, was 90 years old!

Recalls Pam, "To get Joe known in Talladega, we went to anything and everything that was going on. We held meet and greets. We knocked on doors. We even went to a retirement center...those folks really do care about the community. And they vote!"

Joe continues, "I talked to everyone I could. Business owners. The local college president. I wanted to share my vision with them and show them how I could help.

"We also video-taped a lot of the events we attended. We would post the videos on Facebook and that helped tremendously. I think out of the initial 12 ward candidates, I'm the only one who bothered to create a political page on Facebook. When I started this, I had twenty friends on Facebook. Now I have more than 200!"

The actual election Joe was running in, was between him, the incumbent and one other person. Joe Power got more votes than any other candidate. The trouble is, if there are multiple people, you had to have attained at least a 50% result. Joe laments, "I got 49.7%!"

So, the Powers went onto a run-off between Joe and the incumbent. And Joe and Pam both remember, "That's when it got really nasty."

Joe prevailed and beat the other incumbent candidate handily. And life truly changed for the Powers, starting the day after the election. Says Joe, "I'm no longer the 'new guy' in town. People everywhere say 'hello.' Everyone always wants to talk to me. We get invited to *everything*. It's kind of a big ego boost, to tell you the truth!"

But from the get-go, Joe was never in this fight for himself or for his ego. It was to improve and expand the city of Talladega, where he has proud family roots and an appreciation for the city's extraordinary history. Joe feels a lot of gratitude for things he accomplished since the election and has big plans for the future. Already, he has given the people of Talladega access to the City Council meetings by streaming the meetings live on Facebook. And the agenda is now posted on the website so residents can see what issues are being discussed. "Each week," declares Joe, "We have between 600 and 800 people watching the meetings online."

He also has plans for increasing tourism to the area ("There's so much history!") and improving the financial management of the city. "My banking background qualifies me perfectly for this."

Joe Power decided to not retire, but instead to inspire. He and his wife Pam are better for it and so is the city of Talladega. The couple is busier, happier, more energized and more involved than ever. It's proof that at any age, you can elect to make a difference.

And Joe showed he had the power to do just that.

What was the biggest obstacle you faced running for City Council?

Replies Pam Power, "Aside from never running for any position before, the toughest part was that people didn't know Joe as well as his opponents.

Did you have a campaign slogan?

"Yes!" says Joe. "It was *Reasonable People do Reasonable Things.* It sounds kind of hokey, but what was going on in government was very UNreasonable, so I thought that was a good message of what I could bring to the table. My runoff opponent's slogan, and I'm not kidding about this, was *I Am Not a Crook.* That should give you some idea of how crazy things were."

Has your run and win changed your view of politics at all?

"Well, I realized it's certainly no fun when all the negativity is directed at you,' says Joe. "I have to say, it's not a good profession to be in if you can't shoulder that." Pam adds, "You know, Joe is so even-tempered. That kind of stuff doesn't really rattle him. And that really worked to our advantage."

"Coming off of this," continues Joe, "I also feel that everyone should run for a political position once in their life. It's a feeling like no other."

Did you have a big surprise in this whole political experience?

Pam answers, "Well, I go back to Idele, our 90-year old campaign manager. She was so dedicated, and she work so hard. At 90!" Adds Joe, "I didn't know she liked me so much!"

Which Hollywood stars would play you in "Election Power-- The Movie?"

Joe says, Tom Selleck. Pam says, Susan Sarandon. But movie or no movie, in Talladega, Joe and Pam are real celebs.

If you elect to contact Joe, he can be reached at
JoePower4Ward3@msn.com.

This Bud's for You.

How a Multi-Careered, Never-Say-Never 70-Year-Old Ended Up Budtending in Colorado's Largest Marijuana Dispensary.

Linda Kleiman has made many diverse and interesting career choices in her life. But she'd be the first to admit, that in her seventh decade, she's finally gone to pot. Linda is now Budtender, which means she educates and serves customers in a marijuana dispensary. Linda says, "I think I might be the oldest Budtender in Colorado." If not the world…

There is nothing in Linda's past that would have foreshadowed that, as a senior, she would end up working in this recently legalized profession that's dominated by trendy, energetic 20- and 30-somethings. But then again, Linda has pretty much lived her life without much predictability. She says, "I never wanted to wonder what it was like to do something. So, most the time, in my life, if I found a passion, I just jumped in and followed it." Her wildly varied professional resume is proof that she sure did.

Always artistically gifted, Linda's initial career path led her to the ad world. She became a high-level art director and worked for the acclaimed Chicago-based firms J. Walter Thompson and Foote, Cone & Belding. She recalls, "I realized I was a damn fine artist, but I realized I might not be the best in the world. Aha! But I could *use* the best artists in the world to create great things." And she *did* create great things with award winning campaigns for national clients such as Oscar Mayer, Sara Lee and Kraft Foods.

But after nearly 15 years in the crazy-paced, tightly-deadlined advertising business, Linda "hungered" for something sweeter. So of course, she did just what you'd expect an accomplished advertising executive to do: She opened a bakery.

With honesty she says, "I had no idea what I was doing when I first started out. But it was probably one of the best times of my life." Linda fused her baking skills with her promotional talents by designing her own product packaging and website. After 18 glorious years, she faced a crossroad. She sold the bakery and went to work as the marketing director for the large bread company that bought her out. After a few years and a few odd jobs later, she did just what you'd expect an artistically blessed, marketing-oriented, skilled baker would do: She became a personal trainer.

"I had always been a gym rat. But when I turned 60, I decided to take it to the next level and make it my career. I worked at two different Chicago gyms with very different clientele. I think I was the oldest personal trainer there ever was!" says Linda with a laugh. "But I could keep up with the 20-year-olds. Ha! They used to call me 'Sarge.' " And Linda feels she brought a special something to the field. "I had experienced many injuries and surgeries by that point. If I was training someone with bad knees, I knew what that felt like. I knew what a bad back felt like. So, I could relate to older clients the younger trainers didn't quite 'get.' I helped a lot of older people and watched their confidence build. That was really exciting for me."

Although Linda thrived as a personal trainer, life threw in a charley horse. She had to leave Chicago to aid a sick relative. She ended up in a small town in Colorado, where there wasn't really a market for her brand of personal training. There wasn't much of a market for *anything,* as a matter of fact. But there was a "budding" new industry in the state that peaked Linda's interest. It was the cannabis business. "I hardly ever smoked pot. But I said to my husband, I'm going to be a Budtender. He thought I was nuts."

Linda ventured into the Budtender profession on a fancy. But there's nothing casual about mastering the profession at all. It requires plenty of training and a lot of learning…think of the expertise required as that of a wine sommelier. The marijuana dispensaries count on their Budtenders to educate the customers and recommend a variety of products for a variety of needs. Some customers' end goals are purely recreational. But others have medical needs, where the knowledge and understanding of the Budtender becomes crucially important. The dispensary where Linda is works has an entire in-house "university" which offers "robust classroom and experiential training" to the more than 600 employees. Linda adds, "You have to know so much. Just everything. And we have so many products, with new ones coming in all the time. It just blows my mind how much I now know."

The dispensary turf requires a rigorous, ongoing education. But it's an enjoyable one. Says Linda, "It's a gas. It's fun! I mean, this is marijuana. And right now, I work in one of the busiest places in Colorado." Linda says there are constant lines out the door and her and her fellow Budtenders may see as many as 1,000 customers a day. "You meet people from all walks of life. Obviously, everyone's over 21, but you get 80-year-old's coming in. There are all kinds of people you wouldn't expect, all there to buy marijuana. It's just an amazing new industry to be part of."

Linda continues, "You get to know people and form some really good relationships. You start to recognize what they like and you can make recommendations. And they like ME to talk to finicky

customers because I'm older. And I know how to talk to people."
She adds with a smile, "But of course, the customers don't know
how old I am. Because, for the most part, I still like to act like a
goof."

Becoming a Budtender later in life has only enhanced Linda's
youthful outlook, ageless energy and fearless attitude. She says,
"I'm not afraid of too much these days."

Even at the age of 70, Linda Kleiman's career, although yet
another new one for her, is still smokin'. And it doesn't appear
that it or she will burn out any time soon. In her own words:
"Looking back on life, I've really done it all. But I'm not done."
No surprise there.

**What advice would you give someone older about starting a
brand-new career in a youth-filled industry?**

Linda reflects, "If you're thinking of trying something new, just go
for it. You just don't know what you're capable of. You always
have a choice to do something or not to do something. If you
choose not to do it, then you've lost."

**"What does your family think about you working in the
cannabis industry?"**

"My husband says it's his favorite job I've ever had. And he is
especially fond of it when I bring home samples!"

What was the hardest part about starting a new career in the cannabis industry?

Linda says, "Being the newbie, yet again. I didn't know anything about it. But I've had to work my way up from that position so many times in life, I just trusted myself to learn it."

If your life story ever becomes a Hollywood movie, who would play you?

Linda quickly replies, "Gina Gershon. Maybe because she has red hair." Or maybe because Ms. Gershon, like Linda, has a crazy-long and diverse resume (theater, films, TV, music, books) and she's still going strong.

Redesigning Her Life.

***Why Acclaimed Interior Designer Lynn Gendusa Walked Away
from Wallpaper and into Newspapers.***

After wowing Atlantans for 44 years with her amazing interior design skills, Lynn Gendusa was ready to hang up her fabric swatches. Says Lynn, "The last house I decorated was 25,000 square feet. It was my BIG swan song...*really* big. And I was exhausted. I loved my career as a designer. I loved the creativity and I loved my clients." But Lynn was definitely ready for her next chapter. And that change of plans literally ended up being "chapters." In addition to writing hundreds of touching, thought-provoking, sometimes hilarious newspaper columns that are picked up all across the country, Lynn published her first book.

Lynn's later-in-life entrance into the writing world is more a full circle than a full surprise. At age 19, when she was a freshman in college, one professor recognized a writing gift that even Lynn didn't know she had. She recalls, "I had a great English professor named Dr. Fred Freeman. After I handed in my first paper, he took me aside and said, 'You're so talented with your words, I'd like to invite you to a student writing seminar in Connecticut that we attend once a year. It's ONLY for seniors, but I'm inviting you as a freshman.' And I responded, 'No sir, I can't. I'm dropping out of school and getting married.' And I that's just what I did."

Had Lynn gone to Connecticut, maybe she would have pursued a writing career. But instead, fast-forward a bit, she found herself as a single parent with three little mouths to feed. And although she never lost the desire to write, she didn't see it as an immediate way to put food on the table.

To support her family, Lynn went to design school and entered the interior design field. Along with her artistic talents, she brought a unique perspective to the industry. Lynn positioned herself as a single design source for builders, which was a novel idea back in the 1970's. Says Lynn, "I just came up with the idea, 'Why should builders' clients have to many resources to get everything they need? They could just come to me.' It was working really well and I was getting job offers from companies left and right. One offer was a call from a man who said they were building a new company, a home center based in Atlanta, and they would like to bring me on as their on-site designer. I would be one of their first employees. But I didn't like the name of the company, so I said 'No, thanks.' The name was Home Depot."

Four and a half decades later, around the time the last window treatments were being hung in that mammoth design project that would be her last, Lynn would go to bed, exhausted from the day's work. But she couldn't sleep. Stories would start coming into her head. Stories about her childhood in rural Tennessee. Stories about her family and her faith. Stories about struggles and joy. Stories that would make people laugh and others that would make people cry. And she knew she had to let them out. She physically felt someone poking her in the shoulder every night saying, "You promised. You promised." So, one day, mad-as-heck about her lack of sleep and with a big ol' cup of coffee, she went to her computer, sat down and born again was the gifted writer that dropped out of college at 19 years old. And she didn't get up from that chair until she had written her first story…a LONG story. But one thing was immediately clear: Those 2,500 words didn't come from her keyboard. They came from her heart.

"When I finished the story," Lynn says, "I thought who the heck is going to publish this? Newspaper columns are typically 700 words!" But Lynn sent it to the *LaGrange Daily News* anyway, a newspaper based in her old hometown. "Three days later, I got a call that they were publishing that story—in three back-to-back daily issues. Two weeks later, I asked them if they needed a columnist and they did. And, I've been writing weekly columns for them for the past five years."

Although Lynn's columns started in LaGrange, they've grown to be so popular and are so in demand, they're picked up by newspapers everywhere; not just all over Georgia, but all over the country. You can even find her byline in USA Today. Lynn feels part of the reason her popularity has soared is because it's just what the country needs right now: a break from all the arguing and polarization. ("Newspapers need writing that pulls people together, to a warm place, a place of comfort. Right now, people need hope.") Lynn's writings offer encouragement, inspiration and many times, a good belly laugh. They cover a whole host of topics, from family, friends, heartbreak and holidays. They might be about domestic abuse or depression. Or even about "The Healing Power of a Homemade Pie." As she says with true irony, "One day I'm writing about the magic of fried chicken and the next about the tragedy of suicide."

Lynn figures has written more than 250 columns. And was encouraged by everyone to spread their reach even wider by compiling many of them in a book. In 2018, she published *It's All Write With Me! Essays from the Heart.* The book is a beautiful tapestry of life woven together like only Lynn can and, no surprise, receives all five-star reviews on Amazon. Lynn says, "Folks say it's a good bedside table book because you can enjoy any of the stories at random." And they also say it's wonderful.

Lynn is finally enjoying what she was meant to do: She's writing stories straight from her heart that touch people everywhere. She's constantly getting emails and letters from all over the country from people telling her how much a story meant to them or how it changed their life. It's certain, the whole world is glad that Lynn changed *her* life. She did the write thing.

What did your family think about you starting a new career in writing?

They always knew I would do this! No surprise. The surprise was that it exploded overnight. They are very supportive.

Did you get advice from other journalists?

"Lee Walburn, renown columnist and former Editor-in-Chief of Atlanta Magazine, said to me 'Your purpose is this: You make 'em laugh. You make 'em cry. Or you make 'em think. That's your job.' He's a good friend from my hometown of LaGrange, Georgia."

Do you have a mantra or words you live by?

"Yes! 'I hope you take away the knowledge that no matter what you endure, life goes on until the final chapter. When you hear your name being called from way up yonder. Until then, live boldly, beautifully and benevolently.' "

Did anything about your journey to become a successful columnist surprise you?

"Everything about this surprised me! And how fast it all happened."

What do you think is the hardest part about writing your weekly column?

Making sure what I write truly comes from you heart. It has to come from my soul. And sometimes with deadlines and all, it's easy to forget that.

Do you wish you made this decision to be a writer earlier in life?

"No!" Lynn answers definitively. "The stories wouldn't have been as good. I had to go through everything I've lived through to make the stories come to life. I think it turned out just the way it was meant to turn out."

Which Hollywood star would play you in "Lynn Gendusa, the World-Famous Columnist?"

After pondering the thought, Lynn settles on Reese Witherspoon. "She's from Nashville. She 'gets' the whole southern thing. I think she could pull it off." Whether there's a movie made or not, Lynn Gendusa is a blockbuster success.

You can read Lynn's inspiring columns or order her book at www.lynngendusa.com.

And if you need someone to talk to, she's right here: lwgendusa@bellsouth.net.

The Art of Connection.

How a Korean Grandmother and Grandfather Drew Their Family Together and are Still Drawing Admirers All Over the World.

A few years ago, 78-year old, Korean native Chan Jae Lee was not in a good place. Quite literally. He was on the wrong continent.

Grandpa Chan and his wife Marina lived in Brazil. Their daughter, her husband and two young boys, who had lived in Brazil for many years, just moved back to South Korea. The couple's son and his wife lived in New York. Chan, who had adored spending time with his grandchildren, grew lonely. Sad. Inactive. And as his son Ji puts it, "downright grumpy."

Ji and his sister, Miru, were worried about their dad's sedentary lifestyle, mental state and the fact that he was unhealthily glued to the television. So, the siblings brainstormed and thought they would encourage him to start drawing again, an activity he had once enjoyed but had long ago given up, (probably for television). Ji would teach his father how to use Instagram so he could post his drawings every day and possibly build a following. Never mind that Chan didn't even know what Instagram was!

The intention was good, but it didn't work so well. Ji's father was going through the motions of drawing pictures, but he was unenthused. Resistant, even. He had trouble figuring out *what* to draw. And he wanted nothing to do with Instagram.

But then, a wonderful new inspiration entered his life: another grandson was born. Ji and his wife, in New York, had a baby and

Grandpa Chan and Grandma Marina came to meet the new family member. They were overjoyed with baby Astro. Just thrilled and smitten. But there was a moment during that visit when Grandpa Chan became gloomy. He was upset that Astro wouldn't know or remember him when he was older, "Because," Grandpa Chan said sadly, "when Astro is older, I won't be around anymore." The thought truly broke Ji's heart. But it also gave him a life changing idea that would have a remarkable, unpredictable effect on the entire family. The idea was so well-received by so many that these days, Grandpa Chan is ON television, not watching it.

Ji suggested that his father draw daily pictures for his grandchildren. Each day, Grandpa Chan could post them on Instagram for the kids...and the whole world...to see. The illustrations would depict all kinds of things about Grandpa Chan: his daily activities, the story of his hard childhood, local landmarks and Korean customs. Sometimes it could be what he had for lunch or what he saw in the park that day! Some of the pictures could just be entertaining for the children, like colorful animals or imaginary friends. Through the pictures, Grandpa Chan could not only connect with the grandkids daily, he could communicate so much about their family's history and Korean history, in a format the kids could relate to and understand. His collection of daily pictures could be a beautiful, artful legacy he could leave behind. And it could be appreciated by generations to come.

The project would be called "Drawings for my Grandchildren," and Grandpa Chan immediately loved the idea. It brought him energy, enthusiasm, a creative outlet and excitement. Best of all, it gave him a purpose for each and every day. Amazingly, it became very much a whole family project. While Grandpa Chan would do the actual drawings, Grandma Marina grew to be an indispensable part of the venture. She would often select the subject matter, do research and write a story to go along with the picture. Ji would then translate his Grandmother's Korean words into English and his sister Miru would translate the words into Portuguese. The "Drawings for my Grandchildren" project constantly connected the family and in a very special way. Says Grandpa Chan, "Every day we upload the drawings and stories and we have a group discussion. Through this process, we all learn a lot about each other."

The project was conceived to engage Grandpa Chan, but it unexpectedly and astonishingly grew to something much, much bigger. It turns out, it wasn't just the grandkids who loved the drawings and stories, but many (many!) other people did, too. The Instagram account was gaining followers from everywhere. The family started receiving hundreds of messages each month of support and praise. Ji was so pleased how both his father and the project were coming along, he decided the whole effort deserved more recognition. Plus, he wanted to promote this idea of how family generations can and should bond and connect. He produced a charming, heartfelt, 3-minute video that encapsulated the development of "Drawings for my Grandchildren" and posted it on Facebook. The story was so touching and universally appealing, the video went viral. Within a short period, the Instagram account blew up and today has garnered over 400,000 followers and counting. In the words of Ji, "Everything just really exploded." Suddenly, Grandpa Chan and Grandma Marina were known all over the world.

Newspapers, radio stations and magazines got wind of the social media phenomenon and began clamoring for interviews and details. Galleries wanted to put Grandpa Chan's art on display. Consumer brands wanted to partner with the Lees. They were asked to speak at events. And now, quite regularly, Grandpa Chan is sitting on the other side of the TV screen telling his story. He's made many television appearances on both Korean and American

TV. Says Marina, "Drawings for my Grandchildren became bigger than we ever imagined. At age 77, we started a new career!"
Ji is just amazed at what the project did for his parents. "Well, it completely changed their lives," Ji reflects. "They have a purpose every day.

"And they are so much more active. They are doing new things and being expressive and creative. They are constantly stimulated. I believe it's added years to their lives. Plus, their lives are now so much more meaningful. It just makes me so happy that they are so happy."

The drawings from the project have evolved greatly, as has Grandpa Chan. He's not *quite* as grumpy and his artistic aptitude has been meticulously honed. He constantly experiments with different media and unusual canvases such as seashells or stones. His stunning and meaningful Instagram images have been made into posters and are purchased by fans all over the world. A book of the drawings has been published in Korea and will soon be translated to English to be sold in Europe and the United States.

The worldly success of the "Drawings for my Grandchildren" project has given Grandpa Chan and Grandma Marina opportunities they never dreamed they would have. They've traveled around the world presenting exhibitions of their drawings. They have an income that allows them to live independently and well. But most importantly, the project has given them a new spark for living. For proof, just bring up their TikTok account where you can watch the two of them perform the latest dance moves to hip hop music and the likes of Michael Jackson's *Billie Jean*.

Says Ji, "Most of all, I have a deep sense of gratitude that through this project, we all connect as a family and my parents are having the time of their lives. We hope our story is an example and inspiration for seniors everywhere." He adds, "And my father can now use Instagram!" And apparently, he can dance.

Through the sheer ingenuity of "Drawings for my Grandchildren" and the truly beautiful effort of an entire family, Grandpa Chan now finds himself in a very good place.

Do you have any words of advice for any other children trying to engage their parents or grandparents?

Says Ji, "The family around older people can play a big part in keeping them active and healthy. Everyone needs to have empathy and patience. Don't give up. Help them figure out what their new purpose can be. Any family can do what we did. Not necessarily with art, but maybe it's music or cooking…whatever the elder person is passionate about. My parents were passionate about their love for their grandchildren."

What do the children (now four of them!) think of their grandparents??

"My son is very aware of his grandfather's work. My daughter is still too young, "replies Ji. "But my two nephews in Korea are very proud that their Grandparents are semi famous. They see them on TV! Now, they are participating more. They do dance moves on Tik Tok with their Grandparents! That's pretty cool."

What was the hardest part about your family's project?

"The technology part was hard," answers Ji. "My father was not into any kind of social media. He knew nothing about any of it and was resistant to learn."

If the creation of the "Drawings for my Grandchildren" project ever becomes a Hollywood movie, who would play Grandpa Chan and Grandma Marina?

Ji answers, "My father could definitely be played by the crazy father from the movie *Parasite*." The Korean actor's name is Kang-Ho Song. "And my mother could be played by a famous Korean actress that played in a movie called *Mother*. They actually look alike!" He's speaking of actress Kim Hye-ja. Let's just hope those two well-known stars have their hip hop dance moves intact!

**To see more of Grandpa Chan's beautiful drawings, go to
@drawings_for_my_grandchidren on Instagram.**

Chairman of the Board.

How an Acclaimed Research Professor Tabled an Illustrious Academic Career and Started Making Tables. And Chairs. And Cabinets...

In the world of psychology, Dr. Abraham Tesser has a world of accomplishments. He is well respected and well known. He spent 32 years in academia holding a faculty position at the University of Georgia, retiring as a Distinguished Research Professor of Psychology. He made significant contributions in the field of Social Psychology and his research has been supported by impressive names such as the National Science Foundation and the National Institute of Mental Health. Abraham headed influential psychology-based organizations. He published dozens of articles on psychology and edited several books.

So, when Abraham retired, he and everyone around him assumed he would continue to involve himself in the research end of psychology that was his passion for so long. But his life went another way and took an unexpected twist. An *actual* twist. He started bending wood and he loved it.

Abraham Tesser left the world of psychology and became a furniture maker. He has an impressively equipped studio in Athens, Georgia, where he carefully crafts and occasionally sells his award-winning creations. But before you think Rooms To Go[R], think more like The Metropolitan Museum of Art. Abraham's furniture is like nothing you've ever seen. Although his designs are perfectly sturdy and functional, they are unique and stunning sculptures, true pieces of art. The shapes are unexpected. The details are beautiful and intricate. These pieces yearn to be observed; to be touched and to be *experienced.*

Some pieces are themed: designed around religious traditions, facets of nature or paying homage to famous styles of art. Some are put together strictly for fun. Tesser's work can't quite be categorized, but there are hints of Danish modern, Chinese and Japanese influences. One thing you *can* surmise about his furniture is that it is exquisitely unique.

While Tesser puts painstaking hours of thought and planning into each and every piece, the wood itself takes "a starring role." The design may be dictated by the variations in the curly maple, the grain of walnut or the color contrasts in the olive ash burl. Says Abraham, "Much of my work revolves around showing beautiful, sensual wood to its advantage." Although one thinks of wood as a straight material, creating sharp angles, Tesser often sculpts the wood or delicately bends it. Because of that, his table legs may follow a sweeping curve. Chair backs may have an alluring, sinuous wave. Reports Abraham, "I love nonlinear shapes and they are integral to much of my furniture."

Although in earlier years, Abraham toyed with woodworking, it wasn't until after his retirement that he really became immersed. When he was employed by the University, he didn't have the free time to learn and experiment with wood. He admits, "I was a workaholic back then!" But with his newfound freedom, he decided to take some classes in woodworking. Recalls Abraham, "The classes I took changed the kind of woodworking I did. My work became much more sophisticated. I traveled around the country and studied woodworking with some people who I thought did incredible work." Tesser diligently studied, learned and practiced. He truly mastered woodworking techniques. "I got to the point that I wasn't saying can I make this? But instead, what am I going to make? And that's the point when it became really interesting."

With unexpected twists and movement, and the incorporation of story-telling graphics and unusual additions such as fabric, the beauty of Abraham's furniture is hard to describe. But the quality of his craftsmanship is easily recognized and often rewarded. Tesser's work has earned awards at several woodworking exhibitions throughout the southeast. His pieces have often been featured in respected woodworking magazines. Abraham says, "Every now and then something wonderful happens. Almost nothing pleases me more than learning that others appreciate my work."

In the woodworking world, Abraham Tesser has grown to be widely known as a highly accomplished, well-respected authority, much like he was in the field of psychology. And while the two fields seem so starkly different, interestingly, Tesser finds them to be very much alike. He reflects, "What I loved about psychology are the same things I love about woodworking. On the outside, they look like very different things. Psychology is abstract, intangible and sometimes even arcane: Woodworking is concrete, tangible and accessible to anyone. In both cases, however, there is a learning curve. Woodworkers must learn which tools do what; how to use the tools and the properties of wood. In research, one must learn how to collect data, how to use statistics and how to communicate the findings. And, there is joy in mastering both sets of skills. But in both cases, once you have the skills, you're looking for something more. In both disciplines, there is a search for "beauty," whether it be concrete or abstract. It's bringing things together in a new, 'just so' way that gives one a feeling of excitement. I found that to be true of my career as a research psychologist and now as a furniture maker."

After his official departure from the University of Georgia, Abraham Tesser did anything but retire. He mastered a whole new, highly complex skill set in an entirely new field. Today, he is thriving with a renewed sense of energy and creativity. As he did as a psychologist, he is making cherished, well-crafted and beautiful contributions to the world. When it comes to a lifestyle that is enriching, gratifying and fueled with daily inspiration, let's just say, furniture maker Abraham Tesser truly 'nailed' it.

Was there anything that surprised you about becoming a furniture craftsman?

"I'm surprised I'm doing it! I loved psychology. I was good at it. I thought I would continue to do it. But as I spent more time at home, woodworking became seductive and more interesting. And I began to meet so many new people who moved me in this direction. I just didn't anticipate it."

"What does your family think about your craft?"

"Oh, they love it!" Tesser says. "My daughter says, 'Don't you sell anything!' "

What is the hardest part about making furniture?

"I think it's the same thing that's always the hardest part of anything: having a good idea." Well, it may be difficult, but Abraham Tesser has managed to come up with a lot of good ideas. Over the years, he estimates he made more than a hundred pieces of furniture.

Do you have a favorite piece of furniture you made?

"Actually, yes. Whatever piece I'm working on at the moment is my favorite piece."

If your life story ever becomes a Hollywood movie, who would play you?

Abraham replies, "An early Dustin Hoffman. A couple of people have told me that I remind them of him. But that was shortly after he played the degenerate Ratso Rizzo in *Midnight Cowboy*, so maybe I should be worried!"

Says Mr. Tesser, "The piece pictured, 'Girls Night Out,' is a collaboration: The amazing quilted panels by Olena Nebuchadnezzar and the upward curves of the legs never fail to lift my spirits." Learn more about this and other fantastic creations at WWW.TesserFurniture.com.

Photo courtesy of Lilia Tesser.

A Classic Rocker.

How a Retired International Marketing Executive Ended Up
Being One of the Most Prolific Baby Holders in the World.

David Deutchman climbed the corporate ladder at Maidenform Worldwide, Inc. for 41 years. And he truly ended up on top. David started as a salesman but finished as the Senior VP of International Sales. In this position, for his last ten years with the company, he would meet with heads of large corporations and lecture to large groups. He traveled the world, once having three meals in three separate countries, all in one day. It was a grand, enviable and a fairly glamorous corporate existence.

When David retired from Maidenform, he wasn't quite sure what his new focus was going to be. But he never thought that his new life's purpose and all-consuming passion would involve being thrown up or peed on. But that's exactly what happened. He started holding babies and loving every minute of it. Ultimately, he became known as 'The ICU Grandpa.'

Right after retiring, David did some consulting for a short time and then did guest lectures on International Marketing at Georgia Tech and Emory University. David enjoyed doing the guest lectures as the kids were fabulous and he loved working with them. But he felt that "it wasn't occupying enough of my time and I really wanted to contribute more." One day David was in his car, stopped at a light in front of a children's hospital and a second virtual light went off in his head. "I just parked my car and went in. I asked for the Director of Volunteer Services and a week later I was working at Children's Healthcare of Atlanta at Scottish Rite!"

It made perfect sense that David's initial assignment at the hospital was education, as he had been recently involved with schools. He started teaching at the on-site learning center the hospital had set up for longer term, school-aged patients. While doing his job one day, he had two encounters with tearful moms who had children in serious condition at the hospital and they clearly needed a shoulder to lean on. Although he was just a stranger in the hospital hallway, they leaned on David. "They ended up sobbing in my arms. I realized then that I wanted to have a job where I would have contact with the moms as well as the kids."

David's new position talking with the moms, consoling and empathizing with families was interesting and demanding. He learned a lot and made wonderful friends. And every day he left the hospital, he felt he had made a difference and had done something good.

One day, a Neo-natal Intensive Care nurse at the hospital approached him and asked him to do something for her. "She said, 'I have a baby in my unit who is two months old and she has never been seen by her parents. She's always alone. Would you go talk to her?' " David was well aware that the nurses were very busy administering medical care and often couldn't fill in the holes absentee or busy parents would create. David goes on, "I went and talked to the baby. A nurse said, 'Would you like to hold her?' I picked her up and she put her head on my shoulder and I fell in love. That was the end of me," he laughs.

Although David was still very involved in comforting moms and supporting older children, holding babies became his specialty. He somehow had just the right touch and almost always knew how to calm them. In addition to helping families all over the hospital, he became a fixture in the infant ICU unit, offering the nurses and emotionally stressed parents some much needed relief. For nearly a decade and a half, he rocked, he cuddled and he sang--- everything from lullabies, to Tony Bennett to The Beatles. Says David, "I estimate holding over 2,000 babies in my fourteen years there." And that's how The ICU Grandpa was born.

"I would like to say I remember all of my babies," says David. "But I honestly can say I do remember many of them." He remembers abused babies, abandon babies, babies born addicted to drugs. David held babies who showed up in the world weeks, or even months, too early. A few of the babies would never make it home.

Over the years, David was highly adored and vastly appreciated in the hospital. But he was also beloved nationally. His story of nurturing ICU babies has been told in many magazines. The ICU Grandpa has been featured in news segments on ABC and CNN. He's done few TV commercials and received humanitarian awards for his volunteer work. David is sort of an icon on social media with thousands of followers and fans.

David proudly and deservedly held the title of Senior VP of International Sales. But in retirement, and just as proudly, he is known as 'The ICU Grandpa.' He never, in a million years, thought that the last 14 years would have turned out with him earning this moniker.

This post-retirement role was unbelievably rewarding and emotionally fulfilling. What's more, it gave David a new and important purpose—so much so he ended up writing a book about it titled *My New Purpose—A Retiree's Discovery in a Children's Hospital ICU*. David's moving words chronicle his experiences in the hospital, from glorious triumphs to heartbreaking tragedies.

And he pays homage to the remarkable strength, courage and resilience of the families he met.

Working at Children's Healthcare of Atlanta changed David's life. And it certainly changed and enhanced the lives of thousands of others, not only the babies, but the children, parents and hospital staff who he tirelessly served for 14 years. They will be forever grateful for his extraordinary dedication, his enormous compassion and his inherent comforting touch. To them and to people all around the world, David Deutchman truly rocks.

Did anything about becoming The ICU Grandpa surprise you?

"I didn't realize I'd see a side of life that most people never experience and couldn't imagine."

What does your family think about you becoming The ICU Grandpa?

"Oh, they love what I have done. My daughters and my wife are proud of me."

What was the hardest part about being the ICU Grandpa?

"The most difficult thing for me to deal with was the babies who leave the hospital with developmental or physical disabilities. It's really tough. I've held babies who had a tracheostomy (a tube that lets the lungs breathe) as an infant, for instance, and still have it nine years later. It's so very hard on the parents. They have to care for the child 24 hours a day."

Could you have become a "baby whisperer" earlier in life?

"No. I was born in the height of the depression. We were very poor. Because of that, I was always financially insecure. So, in my adult life, I was only focused on work and bringing home a check. After 41 years at Maidenform, I was in pretty good shape. That's why I could volunteer."

What is The ICU Grandpa going to do in the future?

"I'm going to write another book. This one will be more about my earlier life and will really be for me and probably never read by anyone else. I'm looking forward to that."

"Plus, I'm going to continue to stay in touch with 'My Moms,' as I refer to the moms that I have worked with at the hospital over the years. I take them to lunch and keep in touch. I love doing that."

If "The ICU Grandpa" ever becomes a Hollywood movie, who would play you?

David answers, "Well, I would hope George Clooney! All my ICU nurses are going to love that!"

You can buy David Deutchman's book
My New Purpose. A Retiree's Discovery in a Children's Hospital ICU at <u>Amazon.com</u>.

Trail Blazer.

*How Fred R. Jolly stepped onto the Appalachian Trail and into
the accomplishment of a lifetime.*

Fred R. Jolly never met an adventure he didn't like.

He once rode a bull—and not a mechanical one! He bicycled from
coast to coast, in just 27 days. Thirty years after graduating
college, he went back to school and got his Master of Liberal Arts
degree. He traveled the world and traveled the country, most
notably taking a two-and-a-half-year RV road trip with his wife,
visiting every state and all 61 U.S. national parks. Before then, he
had never driven an RV, by the way.

So, it's rather fitting, not long ago, Fred decided to tackle the
famous and overwhelmingly difficult Appalachian Trail. It was
going to be a grueling on-foot trek over 2,190 miles of rugged
terrain that would take more than six months. He planned to do a
"thru-hike", which meant completing the trail from one end to the
other, only stopping to eat and sleep each day. The whole trip, he
would be carrying a whopping 30-40 pounds of supplies on his
back. Only one out of four people who start the hike, finish it.

Because people who knew Fred, also knew of his love of an
adventure, they weren't *that* surprised about his new undertaking.
But the shocking factor in his extremely ambitious endeavor, were
that Fred Jolly had ZERO backpacking experience! And what's
more, he stepped into his Appalachian journey on the day he
turned 62. Fred likes to say, "I left the social security office and
went right to the trail."

Interestingly, Fred's life-changing excursion wasn't something he thought about for much of his life. "Most of the people I met on the trail, especially the older individuals, would say 'I've been wanting to do this for 40 years!' " recalls Fred. "For me, it was never like that. I had heard of the Appalachian Trail, but I didn't know anything about it. I literally stumbled upon it!" When Fred and his wife Laura were on that lengthy cross-country road trip, they stopped at a country store in rural Pennsylvania. Fred saw a map of the area on the wall with a long squiggly line through it. "It was labeled the Appalachian Trail. I said holy cow! It's right here! We were actually right at the halfway point of the trail." On a whim, Fred walked about a mile of the A.T. And then, on that beautiful Sunday morning, inspired by the beauty, and of course the challenge, he stopped in his tracks. "Not knowing anything about the trail, I said you know what?! I'm going to walk this thing from one end to the other." And so, it began.

"I didn't even tell my wife of my plans. I started doing research. I found out that the trail goes through 13 states and was almost 2,200 miles. I read that approximately 3,000 people each year attempt a thru-hike and only 25% are successful…and their median age is 29. Since the trail's inception in 1935, fewer than 750 hikers over the age of 60 completed the mission. And even with all the daunting information, I still wanted to do it! I just wanted to see if I still had enough gas in the tank."

While Fred spent the next four years scouring the websites and blogs of those who had completed the trail, meticulously investigating the optimal hiking equipment and watching YouTube videos about the trail, he never did any backpacking. He did diligently train by going on long, single day hikes, but did not experience multiple-day backpacking training hikes. Although his previous accomplishment of a 27-day bike ride gave him some measure of how much a body can do, he had no idea what it would be like to walk 2,200 miles over a six-month period. When asked about his training regime Fred says, "Honestly, it was just like stepping off the side of the pool into the deep end. And then I was in the water." On his birthday, Fred, by himself, stepped onto the trail.

Needless to say, the experience was grueling. Seemingly endless. Emotional. Uplifting. Filled with unimaginable beauty. And at times, frightening as hell. And Fred discovered, "It wasn't as much about the path, as it was about the people. The relationships you develop with the other hikers is incredible. In shelters or on the trail, you get to know people so well. Everyone is working toward the same common goal. So, a wonderful level of support manifests itself. The people were one of the most wonderful things about the hike."

And as well as Fred bonded with and got to know dozens of fellow hikers, he ironically never knew their real names. As part of the "code" of the Appalachian Trail, people only use their trail names, often created based on experiences on the hike itself. To this day, Fred stays in contact with several of them via email and still only knows them as 'Wingman,' 'Easy Bake' or 'Bumblebee.' But Fred chose his trail name before he started on the adventure. He was 'Santiago,' based on the determined lead character in Hemingway's *The Old Man and the Sea*.

On day 195, accompanied by his wife for the last few miles, Fred made the trek up Mount Katahdin in the state of Maine, which marks the completion of the Appalachian Trail. Few have had the tenacity, the strength and the courage to accomplish such a long and treacherous journey. But Fred Jolly was one of them. In addition to this incredible feat, Fred used his hike to raise money for the National Park Foundation. Through his website, he raised $26,000. He chronicled his trek at: www.athike.jollyoutthere.com.

Says Fred, "People still ask me about my hike, 'Why would you ever do that?" And I always say, 'You know what, I just wanted to lose four or five pounds.' " And then he smiles.

Fred Jolly achieved a rare and remarkable accomplishment at an age where to some, it may have seemed impossible. But Fred was a believer and he also believes in aging without limits. So much so, he's planning his next adventure. "I wanted to do something with water this time. I've ridden my bike across the United States and hiked the Appalachian Trail, and I think it would be really cool to do something with the Mississippi River. So, I've decided to do a 'thru-paddle," where you kayak from source-to-sea. I will start where the Mississippi River begins in northern Minnesota. Then I will paddle the 2,300+ miles to the end of the river where it empties into the Gulf of Mexico. This thru-paddle of the Mississippi will be my completion of a triathlon of sorts, a Super Tri! I'm in the thick of doing research on it now."

By the way, Fred R. Jolly has only kayaked a few times in his life.

Do you have any words of advice for anyone else who might want to take on such a monumental endeavor as thru-hiking the Appalachian Trail?

"Your body and mind can do so much more than you could *ever* imagine. Go for it."

Did anything about your A. T. hike surprise you?

"Well, being able to do it. And being able to accomplish something that was so incredibly challenging, especially at my age and with virtually no experience. The day I stepped on the trail, was the first day of my life I had ever backpacked!

Silly question, but what was the hardest part about your journey?

"Well, being 62, the physical part, in general, was hard. And then, at about mile 500, my knee began hurting from an old high school football injury. Because I was doing a thru-hike and hiking each day, there was no recovery time built in. My knee stiffened up and would swell up. At nightfall each day I could barely bend it. And it was that way for 1,600 miles."

Do you have favorite words you live by or a mantra?

"Yes!" answers Fred with enthusiasm. There are two quotes that are particularly important to me. The first is the last line from Mary Oliver's poem, *A Summer Day*: 'Tell me, what is it you plan to do with your one wild and precious life?' And from the movie *Chariots of Fire*: 'Then where does the power come from, to see the race to its end? From within.' "

"I actually keep a journal of my favorite inspirational quotes. Before I went on the trail, I went through that book and wrote my favorite quotes on a piece of paper. It had everything on it from Tennyson to quotes from *Rocky*. On the hike each night, I would pull that paper out and go through those quotes. It kept me going." Of course, the words from Mary Oliver and *Chariots* were on that list.

If your Appalachian Trail hike ever becomes a Hollywood movie, who would play you?

"Ha! One of my hiking buddies and I actually talked about that on the trail. We both agreed Tom Hanks would be a good one to play me. Heck, he survived the COVID-19 thing. He could survive anything, including the hike."

Check out all the details of Fred's hike at
www.athike.jollyoutthere.com.

A Beautiful Mind(fulness).

How a Miami Senior Learned that Teaching an Ancient Practice was Anything But 'Old School'.

When Linda McKenzie was 14 years old, she had a spiritual awakening of sorts. It wasn't in a sacred setting such as a temple, a church or a mountain top. It was in a middle school gymnasium. But that didn't make her recognition any less profound.

Recalls Linda, "The P.E. teacher was guiding us students through a 'progressive relaxation' exercise. It was kind of a mental body scan from your toes to your head. I was sort of drifting off…and I'll never forget this…I had this sudden awareness that there was a place of stillness inside of me that seemed so pervasive. It was an awareness that I knew then, was something I could always tap into."

This extraordinary realization, a 'mindfulness', stuck with Linda through her life. But it didn't manifest fully until nearly five decades after her initial experience. On the cusp of turning 60, Linda began an intense, meticulous, 10-year journey to refine her own, intentional mindfulness practice. But she didn't stop there. She put herself through hundreds of hours of classroom and online training sessions, she earned qualifications up the yin-yang (not a typo but, appropriately, a Chinese philosophy), she attended retreats and workshops around the country…all to teach the practice of mindfulness. So, she could share the gift she discovered with people everywhere and they could also reap the benefits of the daily ritual that forever changed her life.

"Every now and then, I have to stop and pinch myself and say 'Did I really do this? Did I really take this to this level?' I never thought I'd be a teacher—I never taught *anything* before."

She goes on, "It's taken so much work and discipline. But I have really loved the opportunity to teach mindfulness. I see it as a privilege, that the students in my classes trust me to guide them through the course. I'm truly honored."

Linda's journey began in that Evanston, Illinois gym, but after meeting her husband at college, she moved down to his hometown of Miami. He began a dental practice and she worked as his hygienist. When her kids were born, Linda scaled back her office duties to raise a family. She dug her teeth, instead, into parenting and community leadership.

But when Linda was 59, she faced a terrible turn of events. Her mother, who lived thousands of miles away, developed a long-term illness. "I could not be with her all the time to help her and the frequent, spur-of-the-moment calls to travel to be with her proved exhausting, stressful and of course, profoundly sad. I had a tremendous amount of guilt which caused a lot of stress. I was really in crisis. I was sitting in a library chair in our house and I received yet another call to come care for her. The same stillness and awareness arose in me and I knew then, that I could surrender to the circumstances of my life at that moment, whatever they were with kindness and compassion. I found myself resentful, resistant, sad and weary. But as I continued to sit, again an awareness arose in me and I knew that I just had to simply surrender to the circumstances of my life in that moment. Also, at that time, a friend gave me a book that was essentially about mindfulness." As Linda puts it, "And that's how my path opened to me. My path for the rest of my life.

"After I read the book, I began a daily meditation practice. I read, I listened to different teachers and I took a lot of classroom courses. I was semi-obsessed with the learning. And that went on for years." As Linda delved deeper and deeper into mindfulness education, she discovered a local organization that was aligned perfectly with her well-studied passion. It was called Mindful Kids Miami.

This impactful, non-profit's mission is to improve children's lives by giving them access to mindfulness skills, which can in turn reduce stress and anxiety while enhancing their ability to focus. They approach this by training educators and care givers how to incorporate mindfulness practices in kids' daily activities. Of course, Linda saw the great value in this pursuit and it paired so well with her innate love of children. She wanted to be part of it, so she joined the Board of Directors. Shortly after taking this position, her mentor and teacher, the founder of Mindful Kids Miami and the creator of the Mindful Teachers Training Program, told Linda she, herself, should become a teacher. Linda recalls, "I said, oh I've never been a teacher. I don't know if I'd be good at it. The educator replied, 'Oh you *are* a teacher. You just don't know it yet.' So, with her encouragement, I 'dipped my toe in the water.' And then jumped all the way in!"

These days, Linda is a *lead* teacher at Mindful Kids Miami. She went from being a never-teacher to THE teacher. When she initially got involved the organization, it was a requirement to take a class in Mindfulness-Based Stress Reduction (MBSR), a specific, secular, evidence-based approach to mindfulness brought to western culture by a man named Jon Kabat-Zinn, Phd. He is extremely well-known and globally respected in the mindfulness community and considered the true 'father of mindfulness.' It's no surprise his philosophy and teachings really resonated with Linda, so much so that she spent two years completing MBSR trainings and attending retreats, accumulating the necessary requirements to teach. She became a Qualified MBSR Teacher, guiding adults to recognize their stress and to change their relationship to it. And to cultivate their capacity for fully living in their moment-to-moment experience. It has been fulfilling, even life-changing for her to add this to her teaching repertoire. Says Linda, "I see such powerful changes in people through MBSR. People have such stress and struggle with it. The course and the core practices offer the possibility of a different way of being. And it also gives people a community they can tap into. That's very empowering for them."

Linda has come a long way, both literally and figuratively, from the gymnasium floor. But it was the start of a rewarding, transforming voyage that she continues every day. Her diligent learning has helped her cope with the stresses in her own life. And she is wholly gratified and energized by the positive difference she can make by sharing mindfulness with others, making their world…and the whole world…better for it.

Linda's story proves, that at any age, you can make a difference. And a life-altering change. You just must do as she did, with determination, passion and conviction: Put your mind to it.

What does your family think about you embracing mindfulness and sharing your discoveries with others?

Linda beamingly answers, "Well, my husband and two grown sons have taken MBSR, which says a lot. They're very proud that I have pursued this with such vigor. And when meditation comes up in conversation with their friends, they're proud to say, 'Oh, my mom teaches that!' "

What was the hardest part about becoming a mindfulness instructor and getting your MBSR qualification?

"Remembering that I am a 'facilitator' not a "teacher.""

Has anything about your journey into mindfulness surprised you?

Linda responds, "What continues to surprise me is that, the more I continue this journey, the more interesting it is and the more vital it is for me to keep practicing and teaching."

Do you have a 'mantra' or words you live by?

"Let the beauty of what you love be what you do," Linda says, quoting Rumi.

If your journey to becoming a mindfulness teacher ever becomes a Hollywood movie, who would play you?

"Sally Field," Linda immediately answers. "My whole life, people have told me that I remind them of her. I'd like it to be Charlize Theron. But no one has ever made *that* comparison!"

To make a donation to Mindful Kids Miami, go to their website at <u>mindfulkidsmiami.org</u>

Penny's from Heaven.

How a Worldly Chef Ditched Her Spatula and Developed the Perfect Recipe for Saving Senior Dogs.

British native Penny Miller always loved cooking and loved food. So, it made perfect sense, in her younger years, for her to attend cookery school in London where she received her Cordon Bleu certification. She spent years traveling the world, working for 5-star restaurants, acclaimed hotels and preparing meals privately for well-to-do families. At one point, she even owned her own eatery! And although she enjoyed being in the kitchen and always served her patrons splendidly, her chosen livelihood didn't really serve *her*. She says in the most charming Devonshire accent imaginable, "Being a chef just wasn't 'ticking my boxes'. It was hot and sweaty and someone was always yelling at you. Just like Gordon Ramsey!"

After years in the food industry, Penny put her career as a chef on paws. Real paws. She began following another passion that she had all her life: dogs. She was simply fascinated by the animals. She wanted to rescue dogs and rehabilitate them to be more adoptable. She started her learning, following a well-known behaviorist she had hired to work with one of her family's dogs. Penny studied dogs' conduct and mannerisms diligently. According to her, "somewhat obsessively!" She earned diplomas in Canine Behavior and Psychology and became a professional dog behaviorist.

Over the years, Penny has helped literally thousands of dogs and their owners, first in England and then in the U.S. She took on even the toughest cases and turned them around. Her behavior business grew and many of her clients, both four- and two-legged, considered her a real godsend. But it was later in life, this dedicated, caring canine advocate truly earned her wings. In 2016, she fulfilled a decades-old dream and built a one-of-a-kind, forever-home refuge for senior dogs in Georgia. It's called Frankie and Andy's Place.

It's sort of poetic, that as Penny was getting closer to being a senior herself, her life's focus would turn to elders of a different kind. But her fervent passion for this cause, quite appropriately, developed with age. Just as Penny was getting a footing in her dog behavior business back in England, her husband's job brought the entire family (two dogs included!) over to the U.S. Recalls Penny, "I started volunteering at the local Humane Society a few days a week, just so I could keep learning and keep up my momentum. From some of the cases I saw there, to what I saw at the County shelters, I was appalled at mans' inhumanity to his best friend." The widescale animal abuse and neglect Penny witnessed nearly broke her, to the point where she no longer wanted to go to the shelters. She was so traumatized, she wanted to return to England. She consulted her church's Pastor. He told her, 'God doesn't always put you where you want to be. He puts you where He needs you to be.' For Penny, it was a pivotal moment. She says, "Those words hit me like a train...I literally got goosebumps." Of course, Penny stayed in America.

Another incredibly sad thing that Penny experienced in the shelter was the lack of interest in senior dogs. It was something that made an unbelievably powerful impression on her. "When people would come in for adoption, they only wanted the cute, young, 'chocolate box cover' dogs," says Penny in a very Penny-ish way. "The senior dogs, who gave years of service to their owners, and were cruelly tossed aside because they lost their charm, or started peeing on the carpet in their old age, were never even looked at.

These poor dogs who thought they were going to have a comfy retirement with their families, instead were discarded like trash and put in sterile cages with very little human contact. Sometimes not even a blanket."

Penny was so outraged by this, she was determined to do something about it, at least for as many senior dogs as she could. She vowed that someday, she would find the resources to build a refuge specifically for senior dogs. She would pull them from the shelters and bring them to a warm, wonderful, home-like, sanctuary where they would be loved, nurtured and truly honored in their final stretch of life, but most of all, be given a purpose.
Her driving mission in life is that ALL God's creatures need to work, to have a purpose, to be needed by someone. Therein lies true fulfillment in life.

With the tremendous support of some very encouraging friends, Penny opened a boarding and dog rehabilitation ranch just north of Atlanta. Aside from fulfilling her love of working with canines, the purpose of the business was to make money to fund the senior dog rescue she so vividly envisioned. The journey entailed a lot of hard work, sacrifices and frustrating setbacks. But eventually, after lots of blood, sweat and tears, experiences with thousands of dogs and some magically effective fundraising, ground was broken for a unique, spectacular haven for senior dogs. She named it after two special rescue dogs that held a sacred place in her heart. She called it Frankie and Andy's Place.

Today, 22 senior dogs live in the two, charming, very homey log cabins Penny built especially for them. Describes Penny, "Each cabin is really a home, there's no shelter vibe, there's no tragedy...they actually live better than we do. It's truly the happily-ever-after of dog rescue."

At Frankie and Andy's, there are no cages. The dogs spend their days on soft couches and comfy rugs or in the three-acre woodland yard with fresh air and sun on their face. They are fed wholesome, home cooked food made right there in the kitchen. (Now Penny's a chef with quite a different clientele!) Although they are administered medicine if necessary, they are treated very holistically, with natural substances, for any of their aches and pains. And it's effective! Says Penny, "They live so bloody long when they come to us. They're on their last legs, hobbling through the door when they arrive. And then suddenly, next day they're breakdancing!"

Another reason these dogs unexpectedly thrive at Frankie and Andy's Place is because of the unbelievable level of unconditional love they are given. Penny has a small team of staff and around 40+ incredibly special, very giving volunteers. "Everyone who works here is incredible," beams Penny. "They adore the dogs. They would do anything for them."

Frankie and Andy's volunteers are amazing and generous, but *they* seem to get plenty out of being part of the crew, as well. Reports Penny, "We've had loads of folks come off blood pressure medications, people no longer needing anxiety medications after just a few weeks of volunteering. Our greatest achievements, however, are with our special needs youngsters, one of whom went from being totally non-verbal to 'Chatty Kathy' just because of her 'cabin therapy'." Those dogs work miracles every day.

So far, Frankie and Andy's Place has saved 62 senior dogs. More than 130 volunteers have given of their time. Thousands of others have donated. And Penny is not closing the door any time soon. Later in life, she knew it wasn't too late in life to make a difference. To dogs. To the world.

Penny Miller is truly an angel. And of a breed all her own.

Where did the name "Frankie and Andy's Place" come from?

"During my time volunteering at the Humane Society, I walked into the shelter and there was this dirty, skinny, sickly Great Dane who had been found abandon and tied to a tree for two weeks. His name was Frankie", recalls Penny. "Our eyes locked, and I said 'Whoa'. I had to take him home. (But the two of us stopped at McDonald's first so I could start fattening him up!) He went on to live to 12 years---a very long life for his breed. Andy was another resilient dog, rescued from a shelter and went on to live to 16. Our beautiful senior sanctuary was built in their presence and their honor."

What was the hardest part about creating Frankie and Andy's Place?

"The sheer time it took. I was also running a boarding and behavioral business which was 60 hours a week. It took me away from my family quite a bit and that was hard."

Has anything about having Frankie and Andy's Place surprised you?

Note: Penny wells up with tears of gratitude when answering this question.

"Honestly, it's the people.

"I had grown to hate people. After seeing what they do to dogs, how they treated them like trash. At Frankie and Andy's Place, I now see the amazing good in people. The volunteers all see the dogs as family. They embrace the dogs like their own children. Now, I see the very best in people rather than the worst. I really didn't think I'd feel that way again."

You found your 'purpose' later in life with Frankie and Andy's Place. What purpose do you give your senior dogs?

Replies Penny, "What we do defines us, gives us a reason to get up every morning. The dogs at the cabin are no different to humans in that regard. All of them, every single one of them, wakes up in the morning knowing that they have to put their healing hats on and help to change the world. And they do it brilliantly.

"For some of them, it might be that they visit assisted living facilities, where they are held and nuzzled by folks who are not able to have pets, but were desperate for that non-judgmental, easy interaction once again. Others go to the memory care units, where otherwise confused Alzheimer's patients become surprisingly lucid and talkative, fond memories returning, when holding one of our senior dogs.

"Yet others go to one of the three schools we visit every week, to work with special needs children in the classroom. For four years, our senior dogs have visited an adult day care center every week without fail, where they work gently and affectionately with physically and mentally handicapped adults, who touch and stroke them, sometimes even walk them under guidance.

"The 'healing paws,' well, that speaks for itself when you read about the work that these golden oldies do in the community."

If "Building Frankie and Andy's Place" ever becomes a Hollywood movie, who would play you?

"I know who I would *want* to play me, it would be Eva Mendez. But the truth is, it's more likely to be Kathy Bates."

Donations to Frankie and Andy's Place would be very gratefully received at <u>frankieandandysplace.org</u>.

Write On.

Why a Longtime Copywriter Decided to Not Wind Down Career-Wise, But 'Book It' Instead.

(About the Author, By the Author.)

I've always been pretty lucky.

I was one of those people who was lucky enough to find out what I wanted to do with my life, early in life.

I was lucky to nab a college roommate who encouraged me to try an Intro to Advertising class and I was immediately sold. She obviously was innately good at advertising. After graduation, in a tough job market, I was fortunate to be hired as a copywriter at JWT in Chicago. Because of too much snow and too cold temperatures, I transferred to JWT Atlanta where I continued to grow my career along with growing a great marriage (Lucky!) and four awesome kids. (Lucky again.)

I loved my advertising career. I got the opportunity to write about Kraft Mayonnaise, Oscar Mayer Hot Dogs, Dunlop Golf Balls and even Cabbage Patch Kids. But later in life, as I moved away from the big ad agency life and did freelance writing for more local entities, I got lucky again. I started working, as a contractor, for a huge and impressive Atlanta retirement community in their marketing department. In addition to direct mail pieces, brochures, etc., I was assigned the utterly joyous job of interviewing the residents of the community and write their life stories. These were interesting, high achieving and still, very active people. I not only fell in love with doing this, (and quite frankly, fell in love with many of these wonderful people, too) I was motivated to do more. As one septuagenarian said to me, "You know, I still have a lot of gas left in the tank." I thought, 'You got that right, girl. Me too.'

I sought to find more people who were turning retirement into *inspirement*. (I made that word up, btw, as I tend to do.) And boy, did I find a bunch of winners: extraordinary people who, maybe because of more free time and less financial obligation, chose to do what they love, later in life. What they've done has made them "younger". Happier. More fulfilled.

And like them, here I am. Later in life, composing a book--- something I've never done.

Writing *Late Boomers* has been an eye-opening, energizing, beautiful journey. I've stretched. I've grown. And just like the incredible people who are profiled in these pages, I discovered, that no matter what your age, accomplishment never gets old.

Lucky me.

Has anything about becoming an author surprised you?

"Yes! The people who I have interviewed have been so generous with their participation and their time. I was shocked, people, most of whom didn't know me at all, willingly jumped right in.

"The other thing that surprised me is that there are so many *Late Boomers* out there! Quite frankly, they weren't that hard to find. Which I think says a lot about the Baby Boomer generation and how ambitious and vibrant they are."

What was the hardest part about writing a book for the first time?

"Well, shockingly, because I've self-published and had no real deadlines, discipline was not hard. I couldn't wait to write these stories.

"The technology of self-publishing was the most challenging part---formatting and such. But my husband was GREAT help."

What does your family think about you writing a book, later in life?

"Oh, they are so great. My husband, who is always encouraging in general, was totally behind the project. My oldest son, Max, helped tremendously with the marketing and the Facebook presence. Like I said, pretty lucky in the family area."

If your journey writing *Late Boomers* is ever made into a Hollywood movie, who would play you?

"Diane Keaton. I don't think I'm quite as 'spacey' as *Annie Hall*, but my husband might disagree."

My wonderful family, (starting left) Sawyer, Elliot, Max, husband Louie, Spencer and me. In their birth order, the kids' initials spell M.E.S.S.

If you have a Late Boomers story, let me know and I'll tell the world! Contact me at Jeri@LateBoomersRock.com

Made in the USA
Columbia, SC
18 May 2021